THE Portable Mentor

THE Portable Mentor

A Resource Guide for Entry-Year Principals and Mentors

Frederick A. Lindley

Foreword by John C. Daresh, Author of *Beginning the Principalship*

CORWIN PRESS, INC.
A Sage Publications Company
Thousand Oaks, California

For information:

Corwin Press, Inc.
A Sage Publications Company
2455 Teller Road
Thousand Oaks, California 91320
www.corwinpress.com

Sage Publications Ltd.
6 Bonhill Street
London EC2A 4PU
United Kingdom

Sage Publications India Pvt. Ltd.
B-42 Panchsheel Enclave
Post Box 4109
New Delhi 110 017 India

Printed in the United States of America

Library of Congress Cataloging-in-Publication Data

Lindley, Frederick A.
The portable mentor : a resource guide for entry-year principals and mentors / by Frederick A. Lindley.
    p. cm.
Includes bibliographical references and index.
ISBN 0-7619-3838-9 (Cloth) — ISBN 0-7619-3839-7 (Paper)
    1. School principals—In-service training—United States—Handbooks, manuals, etc. 2. Mentoring in education—United States-Handbooks, manuals, etc. I. Title.
LB1738.5.L56 2003
371.2'012'07155--dc21

                              2003005455

This book is printed on acid-free paper.

03 04 05 06 07 7 6 5 4 3 2 1

Acquisitions Editor:	Robert D. Clouse
Editorial Assistant:	Jingle Vea
Production Editor:	Julia Parnell
Copy Editor:	Teresa Herlinger
Typesetter:	C&M Digitals (P) Ltd.
Indexer:	Jeanne Busemeyer
Cover Designer:	Tracy E. Miller
Production Artist:	Lisa Miller

CONTENTS

FOREWORD

An amazing thing happened about twenty years ago. People discovered the principalship as a key ingredient in the creation of more effective schools. Actually, virtually anyone who ever worked (or perhaps even visited) a school knew this fact. Simply stated, there is a great deal of difference between an effective school and one that is not serving the needs of students, and much of that difference can be attributed to the ways in which the school is led, whether the leader is a principal, head teacher, or any other title used to describe the leader of an individual campus.

As this reality concerning the importance of principal leadership has seeped into the terrain of educational reform, so too has the recognition that if we want effective principals as leaders, we have to do something to ensure that more people will be successful in their careers. That fact has served as the focus of attempts made during the 1990s to begin to identify more precisely what is to be expected of principals who will "make a difference" in their schools. For a while, it was popular to state only that "effective principals are instructional leaders" and let it go at that. This was a wonderful slogan that allowed people to feel as if they had really discovered something that would be a key to unlocking the mysteries of successful practice in education. But slogans have a short shelf life, and after a while, just what that term meant in reality became more and more obscure. For example, did it mean that principals should spend all of their time visiting classes to observe teachers? Did it imply that principals should begin to teach again? Did it mean that campus administrators would be expected to do more inservice work in their schools? And what about all the other things that principals had to do? How would that be reconciled with the instructional leadership vision?

In response to this need to bring about greater clarity to the forging of a new and better world for school principals, we witnessed the creation of many programs that were designed as a way to pinpoint more precisely what it was that we wanted our school leaders to do. Among the most ambitious was the work sponsored by the Council of Chief State School Officers who worked to articulate a vision of more effective school leadership that could be adopted across the United States. This vision is the foundation of what is now known as the Interstate School Leaders Licensure Consortium (ISLLC) Standards, a set of six principles that are intended to give greater definition to the formerly vague notion of principals serving as "instructional leaders." The ISLLC Standards represent an excellent beginning point for further reform and renewal of school-based leadership across the country. However, the statement of broad principles does little to actually change practice.

Fortunately, a few states, including North Carolina, Texas, Mississippi, and Arkansas, among others, have embraced the newly identified standards that now serve as the basis for licensing and certification of school leaders. And some states, notably Missouri and Ohio, have moved their reform efforts even further by developing new programs and practices that will assist principals and others with the adoption to the new vision of educational leadership for their work in schools. Despite all of these fine efforts, however, a major hurdle still has to be addressed as we try to get a better understanding of what the elusive concept of the "principal as an instructional leader" really means. And that is where a book such as the one you are about to read comes into the picture.

In this book, Fred Lindley provides a coherent description of how to address that gap between theory and practice found so often in discussions of how to improve practice in schools. Through the lens of principal professional development, he provides us with a concrete vision of what the beginning principal needs to do to carve a path in the direction of serving not only as a survivor building administrator but, more important, as a principal intent upon providing her or his school with a vision for the future, along with a plan for the present. This book takes a very strong stance in favor of supporting the instructional leadership of the school principal, but it does so in a way that breaks away from the traditions of the rhetoric that has filled the world of principal literature for the past two decades. And it goes several steps beyond simply restating the ISLLC (and other similar standards now in vogue) vision by providing a bridge between the abstract and the reality of daily work as a school principal. Lindley never forgets that the strength of one's performance as an effective school principal is always a bit of a balancing act between the creative process of building a vision and the daily demands of maintaining order and keeping the ship afloat.

Without much question, the fact that principal leadership is a key ingredient in an effective school carries with it the cost of ensuring that ordinary people who get the job of administrators can actually do the job. This book will provide a great foundation to make that extraordinary task doable.

—John C. Daresh
University of Texas at El Paso
November 2002

FOREWORD

School districts across the country face the increasingly difficult challenge of recruiting talented educators into the principalship. Furthermore, the stress level continues to rise, and burnout among new principals often leads to a high turnover rate, thus aggravating the problem. School principals are facing huge challenges from many directions. The public expects more from schools than ever before, including better school-community relations, higher test scores, positive school climate, equal opportunities for all students, and accommodations for students with disabilities. The need for principals who have the skills and training to accept such challenges has never been greater. Principals are expected to carry out their duties and fulfill their multiple roles flawlessly throughout the day. They must excel as managers, instructional leaders, public relations specialists, community liaisons, and problem solvers. Professional training materials are needed to help educators who are preparing for administrative positions and first-year principals who are struggling to survive the tribulations of the "rookie" principal.

This book is designed to help both groups understand the complexities of school administration in today's society through the presentation of key professional standards and competencies grounded in reality and the practical understanding of these standards in real-life situations. The author has incorporated the six Interstate School Leaders Licensure Consortium (ISLLC) Standards in all four parts of the book. In fact, the content and methods of this book are rooted in the six Standards. I have found both in my classroom and in my administrative workshops that these materials work for school leaders. In every evaluation, participants rated the materials as outstanding, supportive, creative, and helpful. The content in this book, being so closely aligned with the ISLLC Standards, is grounded in reliable research and theory and provides specific suggestions for applying that knowledge to practice. As one first-year principal said, "I referenced the materials on a weekly basis. I would have liked a mentor, but having this notebook was the second-best thing."

Many of the first-year principals will tackle this very difficult position with little or no support; they will not have "live" mentors. The author's use of the first person in this book will enable them to read this text with the feeling that the "portable mentor" understands their situation and has provided wise counsel in tackling the important issues.

I recommend this book for principal preparation courses, mentor programs, and district administrative inservices. By correlating a principal entry-year task list with the ISSLC Standards, the author is able to demonstrate the connection between the day-to-day activities of the school principal and the overarching validity of the national Standards. The book is designed to provide opportunities for students and administrators to sit in the principal's chair and address the situations and problems that they will likely encounter on a daily basis. The scenarios and discussion prompts in Part IV will be particularly helpful to school superintendents as they guide newly appointed principals in addressing leadership issues within districts.

—Timothy J. Ilg, Ph.D., Assistant Professor
Department of Educational Leadership,
University Of Dayton (OH)
November 2002

PREFACE

Let me begin my overview of *The Portable Mentor* by telling you what this book is *not*. This is not an educational textbook, replete with philosophy, conceptual frameworks, and research studies. An abundance of such material exists, much of which, I presume, you encountered as you completed your preparation courses.

Now, allow me to tell you what this book *is*. Originally, I designed this book as a practical, "nuts and bolts" resource for new principals. Later, I added material for people who were mentoring new principals for the first time. In its present form, this book serves those two primary target groups—first-time principals and first-time principal-mentors. In addition, while field-testing this material, I learned that it also assists two other groups of educators—individuals who are exploring the idea of becoming a school principal and students enrolled in preparatory programs, in pursuit of their principal licenses. Some students reported that upon finishing their preparatory programs, they used the content in this book to prepare for job interviews.

The book stems from my continuing passion for the principalship and my desire to help those who assume the role as the school leader. My first formal opportunity to assist beginning principals occurred when I retired from a 34-year career as a building principal and assumed a principal-mentoring role. In the seven years since that initial mentoring experience, I codesigned a principal development project at the University of Dayton, which subsequently became an Internet-based, distance-learning program. That project led to my serving as a regional coordinator with the Ohio Principals Entry-Year Program, sponsored by the Ohio Department of Education. Concurrently, I have written curriculum for, and served as a trainer of, principal-mentors in the O.D.E. Program.

Unabashedly steeped in practicality, this handbook serves primarily as a portable and prescriptive resource for entry-year principals. It provides a focused, organized approach that helps the novice school leader maneuver through the management and organizational demands of the job. Yes, I used the "M" word, "management." While I have no quarrel with the current emphasis on the importance of principals being effective leaders, I maintain that effective leaders must also be effective managers. If they are not, they will not survive on the job long enough to do much leading.

By now, you may have noticed that I am delivering the content of this book in the first person. This "from me to you" style of writing is the personal approach that I prefer. I hope that my attempt to "converse on paper" will give you the sense that I am serving as a mentor to those of you who are first-year principals and a peer to those readers who are serving as principal-mentors. In this way, I hope that you can imagine the two of us sitting together discussing the great adventure of being a first-year principal or first-time principal-mentor.

I have organized the content of this book into four parts: The first three parts, Defining the Job, Doing the Job, and Deciphering the Job, address issues related to the entry-year principal. The fourth part focuses on principal-mentoring issues. Here is a brief overview of each part:

• Part I (Defining the Job) focuses on the importance of developing a conceptual model of the principalship. This part includes information about the ISLLC Standards, which you can use as a conceptual model of the principalship.

• Part II (Doing the Job) provides a chronological listing of tasks that principals encounter during the course of the school year, from preparing to open the school, through the first day and week of school, to the closing of school and getting ready for the following year. The chronological perspective presents a traditional fall-to-spring, nine-month school year. With minor adjustments, persons engaged in year-round school programs will find the content applicable to their situation.

• Part III (Deciphering the Job) presents a list of generalized conclusions and "lessons learned" that have broad-based application to the challenges of being the school leader.

• Part IV (Mentoring the Mentor) addresses issues that a first-time principal-mentor should consider. While the content focuses on the principal-mentor, I encourage the beginning principal to read and draw upon the information in this part.

To the entry-year principal, I want to stress that I do not presume that my written thoughts can substitute for the human touch. If you have access to the services of a knowledgeable, competent mentor, then you are fortunate; many beginning principals do not have mentors. However, even if you do have a mentor, it is doubtful that he or she can be constantly available. *The Portable Mentor* is available whenever you want to take advantage of it. You can carry it with you and refer to it at times and places of your own choosing. You can use it to plan and meet your short- and long-term administrative responsibilities in an organized fashion. I trust that you will find the ideas and material in this book to be helpful as you plan for and conduct the activities that are associated with the school principalship.

To the first-year principal-mentor, I presume that the material in the first three parts of this book will be very familiar to you. Drawing from your experience as a school administrator, your strength will be in helping your mentee interpret and apply the content of this book to the mentee's workplace. Together, I trust that you and I can help the beginning principal succeed and grow on the job. I also hope that the content in this book (especially Part IV) will help you succeed and grow as a principal-mentor.

ACKNOWLEDGMENTS

This book is a culmination of knowledge and experiences accumulated during my 36 years as teacher and school principal and seven subsequent years of mentoring entry-year principals and training entry-year principal-mentors. I am indebted to so many people who helped me during that 43-year time period. Foremost in my thoughts are the teachers, staff members, and fellow administrators who helped me learn on the job and meet my responsibilities. They contributed significantly to my personal and professional growth, and I willingly avow that I was fortunate to be associated with so many capable and dedicated colleagues.

Numerous individuals deserve special recognition. First, I thank my parents, Albert and Bernice Lindley, for their lifelong guidance and support. I am eternally grateful to Carl Garnett, who launched my administrative career by selecting me for my first principalship at the age of 24. John Hoyle, Nick Georgiady, Sam Wiley, and my advisor, Orval Conner, enriched my graduate work at Miami University of Ohio. I owe a special debt of gratitude to two Centerville (Ohio) school superintendents—Donald Overly, who selected me as principal of the Hadley E. Watts Middle School, and Frank DePalma, who, upon my retirement, appointed me to my first role as principal-mentor. I thank Jim Rowley, who connected my mentoring work in Centerville Schools with the University of Dayton, which led to my association with the Ohio Department of Education: O.D.E.: EYP Entry-Year Program. Dan Hoffman, director of the OPLA: EYP, has engaged me in numerous principal-mentoring experiences for which I am most appreciative.

Several individuals at the University of Dayton deserve mention. First, I embrace the memory of the late Joe Rogus, whose wisdom and kindness guided me well, even though our time together was much too brief. I also thank Dan Raisch, who so pleasantly shared experiences and material. I extend appreciation to Father Joseph Massucci and Dean Tom Lasley for enabling me to participate in several principal development activities, including my work with Tim Ilg as we developed an Internet-based distance-learning program for principal licensure. Additionally, Tim's encouragement was central to the completion of this book and his friendship remains priceless.

Corwin Press gratefully acknowledges the contributions of the following reviewers:

Dennis R. Dunklee, Ph.D.
Educational Leadership
Graduate School of Education
George Mason University
Faifax, VA

Edward J. Drugo
Principal
Latrobe Elementary School
Latrobe, PA

Dr. Peggy H. Thompson
Department of Educational Leadership
Mississippi State University
Mississippi State, MS

Gary Crow
Professor
Department of Educational Leadership & Policy
University of Utah
Salt Lake City, UT

Dr. Carmon Weaver
Research Associate
Educational Evaluation Success Center
University of Cincinnati
Cincinnati, OH

Dr. Marc D. Casavant
Department of Educational Administration
University of Saskatchewan
Saskatoon Saskatchewan
CANADA

About the Author

Frederick A. Lindley is an adjunct instructor at the University of Dayton. He has worked in higher education for the past seven years, following a 36-year career (34 years as a school principal) in Ohio public schools. During the past five years, Dr. Lindley has served as the Coordinator of the Southwest Region of the Ohio Department of Education "Entry-Year Principal" program, which entails mentoring new principals, while guiding them toward the completion of performance-based portfolios that comply with the ISLLC Standards. Dr. Lindley also serves as the project's chief writer of curriculum for training principal-mentors. In addition, he works as a writer and web designer for the distance-learning Principal Licensure program at the University of Dayton. Dr. Lindley received his Ph.D. from Miami University of Ohio.

To paraphrase the words of several people who know me well,
I dedicate this book to "the best thing that ever happened to me."
Deborah Kelly Lindley
Best friend, companion, wife, and fellow educator

PART I

Defining the Job

Which Way Is North? 1

Do you possess a definition of the principalship? Should you have one? If "yes," why should you have one?

You may be tempted to brush aside these questions—after all, as an entry-year principal, you completed the course work, you passed the qualifying tests, and the district leadership selected you for the job. You probably feel the need to start working on the tasks that warrant your attention as the new principal. Why spend time on something that appears to be such an academic exercise?

Well, to make this a bit more practical, let us assume that early into the school year, during your goal-setting conference, your supervisor poses the same question. Or, in a different scenario, a news reporter interviewing you as the "new principal" could ask you to list what you see as the most important aspects of being a school leader. Possessing a personal definition of the principalship may take on more relevance under such circumstances.

More important, your personal definition of the principal's role is crucial to your performance as the school leader. If you do not define the job, the job will define you. If you do not have priorities that guide how *you* decide to spend *your* time and energy, others will spend your time and energy for you.

No, you cannot operate in a vacuum, doing only the things that you prefer. You will find yourself expending a considerable amount of time attending to the wants and needs of others. For example, unless you are independently wealthy and can tender your resignation whenever you choose, your decisions about how to spend your time may become more amenable to others than you anticipate. If you need to keep your job and your boss wants the window shades in all classroom windows pulled to a certain level at the end of each school day, you may find yourself revising your definition of the school leader's role to include such a detail. Additionally, there are always those emergencies, or other interruptions, that annihilate your best attempts to be organized and in control of your activities. Without possessing some core beliefs about the role of the school principal, you risk having your day, your week, even your career as a school leader driven primarily by unexpected events and the agendas of other individuals and groups. You must balance the real with the ideal—integrating the realities of your job, shaped primarily by the people with whom and for whom you work, with your personal perspective on how principals should provide school leadership.

What is this "school leadership" that you are to provide? Through the years, numerous experts have conducted exhaustive studies and expressed an incalculable number of words in an attempt to define leadership. Chief among these efforts has been the study of leader traits, leader behaviors, contingency and situational theories, leader effectiveness through power and authority, and, more recently, leading through coaching or influencing others toward accomplishing personal and organizational goals.

Some writers choose to define leadership by distinguishing it from management, one notable researcher asserting that leaders focus on doing the right thing, whereas managers attend to doing things right (Bennis, 1989). I maintain that effective school principals, in part because they are the epitome of middle management, must do both—lead, by doing the right things, and manage, by doing things right. To achieve a gestalt that blends the two functions into a seamless performance of duty, I commend to you the "Head, Heart, and Hand" concept, which Sergiovanni offers in response to the question, "What is leadership, anyway?" In a discussion about the reinvention of leadership, the author asserts that the heart shapes the head, which in turn drives the hand; that is, what you value and believe (in your heart) influences your perspective (in your head) of how the world works and that drives your decisions, actions, and behaviors (through your hands). Sergiovanni emphasized the subtle significance of our subconscious mind set, observing that, "The mental pictures in our heads about how the world works—are often tacitly held. They program what we believe counts, help create our realities and provide a basis for our decisions" (Sergiovanni, 1992, pp. 7–8).

To conclude, only you can answer the question posed at the opening of this module about whether you possess a definition of the principalship. However, I have suggested answers to the other questions posed: Yes, a definition of the principal's role is important to possess, because it helps you stay on course. It serves as your compass; it provides direction. It reminds you "which way is north."

How Do You Organize 2 the Contents of Your Garage?

Perhaps the title of this module should be, "*Do* you organize the contents of your garage?" If not, then I hope there is some aspect of your life in which you demonstrate a skill for organization, for the ability to put things in some sensible arrangement is an important administrative skill.

The sense of organization springs from a mental image of how to arrange different elements systematically. To use the example of organizing the contents of a garage, you could group the hand tools in one area, the lawn equipment in another, the paint supplies in a third, and so on. Alternatively, you could place the contents of the garage in categories of the seasons, thus you store the lawn fertilizer in the summer section, the leaf blower in the fall section, and the snow shovel in the winter section. There are different ways to organize the contents of a garage and each one works to a certain degree.

The same is true about organizing or conceptualizing the various roles and responsibilities of the principal. Given enough time, you and I could develop a lengthy list of issues that a principal must address. Then we could sort and rearrange the different items into an organized schematic or framework, that is, a mental map of the job.

Your mental map of the principalship is critical, because it not only defines the job—*it defines you*. Your image of the principalship, your vision of the school leader's role, and your beliefs about how you think you *should perform* influence how you *will perform*. Possessing a "big picture" of the job can help you stay focused on broad-based, educationally sound priorities. Without such a focus, the pressures or forces from particular areas can be so great that you can lose perspective. You can spend an inordinate amount of time on a few areas that exhibit urgent demands and unintentionally neglect other areas of major importance.

Before going any further, I invite you to use the space at the end of this module to record what you perceive as the ten most important areas of the principalship. Without looking at any resources (no textbooks, no evaluation instruments, no magazine articles, nothing!), list what you perceive as the major performance areas for a building principal.

The next module provides a framework, or conceptual model, of the principalship that I recommend to you. After you have read the module on the ISLLC Standards, you may find it interesting and enlightening to return to this page and compare your list of principal's responsibilities with the ISLLC framework that follows.

The Principal's Major Areas of Responsibility

1. _____
_____
_____
_____
_____
_____

2. _____
_____
_____
_____
_____
_____

3. _____
_____
_____
_____
_____
_____

4. _____
_____
_____
_____
_____
_____

5. _____
_____
_____
_____
_____
_____

6. _____
_____
_____
_____
_____

7. _____
   _____
   _____
   _____
   _____
   _____

8. _____
   _____
   _____
   _____
   _____
   _____

9. _____
   _____
   _____
   _____
   _____
   _____

10. _____
    _____
    _____
    _____
    _____
    _____

3 Will These Six Standards Work for You?

In the two previous modules, I asked you to think about defining the principalship—developing a mental framework for your perspective of the principal's major responsibilities. Now I invite you to investigate the ISLLC *Standards for School Leaders* (Council of Chief State School Officers, 1996), and I encourage you to consider adopting them as your framework of the principalship.

As you progress through this book, you will see that I reference the ISLLC Standards for a considerable amount of material. In Part II, "Doing the Job," I integrate the Standards into the entry-year principal's task list, and in Part IV, "Mentoring the Mentor," I present mentoring material that utilizes the Standards. Given this emphasis on the ISLLC Standards, they warrant further explanation here.

In 1996, after two years of study, the Interstate School Leaders Licensure Consortium (ISLLC) adopted six standards for school leaders. The consortium worked under the auspices of the Council of Chief State School Officers (CCSSO) and in collaboration with the National Policy Board for Educational Administration (NPBEA), twenty-four states, and nine associations representing the educational administration profession. Identifying desirable knowledge, dispositions, and performances of school leaders, the Standards draw upon the research that links leadership and productive schools with significant social and educational trends (CCSSO, 1996).

Six principles guided the development of the ISLLC Standards (Murphy, 2002):

- they anchor on outcomes, rather than functions or tasks
- they focus on student learning and success for all students
- they shift from management and administration to learning and school improvement
- they underscore the collaborative nature of school-based leadership

- they establish an integrated and coherent framework for action
- they shape and direct action for those who are in position to reshape the principalship

The remaining pages of this module list the ISLLC Standards, with their respective knowledge, dispositions, and performance indicators. To find more information about the ISLLC Standards or the CCSSO, visit the following Web site: http://www.ccsso.org/isllc.html

ISLLC STANDARD 1

A school administrator is an educational leader who promotes the success of all students by facilitating the development, articulation, implementation, and stewardship of a vision of learning that is shared and supported by the school community.

Knowledge

The administrator has knowledge and understanding of

- learning goals in a pluralistic society
- the principles of developing and implementing strategic plans
- systems theory
- information sources, data collection, and data analysis strategies
- effective communication
- effective consensus-building and negotiation skills

Dispositions

The administrator believes in, values, and is committed to

- the educability of all
- a school vision of high standards of learning
- continuous school improvement
- the inclusion of all members of the school community
- ensuring that students have the knowledge, skills, and values needed to become successful adults
- a willingness to continuously examine one's own assumptions, beliefs, and practices
- doing the work required for high levels of personal and organizational performance

Performances

The administrator facilitates processes and engages in activities ensuring that

- the vision and mission of the school are effectively communicated to staff, parents, students, and community members
- the vision and mission are communicated through the use of symbols, ceremonies, stories, and similar activities
- the core beliefs of the school vision are modeled for all stakeholders
- the vision is developed with and among stakeholders
- the contributions of school community members to the realization of the vision are recognized and celebrated
- progress toward the vision and mission is communicated to all stakeholders
- the school community is involved in school improvement efforts
- the vision shapes the educational programs, plans, and actions
- an implementation plan is developed in which objectives and strategies to achieve the vision and goals are clearly articulated
- assessment data related to student learning are used to develop the school vision and goals
- relevant demographic data pertaining to students and their families are used in developing the school mission and goals
- barriers to achieving the vision are identified, clarified, and addressed
- needed resources are sought and obtained to support the implementation of the school mission and goals
- existing resources are used in support of the school vision and goals
- the vision, mission, and implementation plans are regularly monitored, evaluated, and revised

ISLLC STANDARD 2

A school administrator is an educational leader who promotes the success of all students by advocating, nurturing, and sustaining a school culture and instructional program conducive to student learning and staff professional growth.

Knowledge

The administrator has knowledge and understanding of

- student growth and development
- applied learning theories
- applied motivational theories
- curriculum design, implementation, evaluation, and refinement
- principles of effective instruction
- measurement, evaluation, and assessment strategies
- diversity and its meaning for educational programs
- adult learning and professional development models

- the change process for systems, organizations, and individuals
- the role of technology in promoting student learning and professional growth
- school cultures

Dispositions

The administrator believes in, values, and is committed to

- student learning as the fundamental purpose of schooling
- the proposition that all students can learn
- the variety of ways in which students can learn
- lifelong learning for self and others
- professional development as an integral part of school improvement
- the benefits that diversity brings to the school community
- a safe and supportive learning environment
- preparing students to be contributing members of society

Performances

The administrator facilitates processes and engages in activities ensuring that

- all individuals are treated with fairness, dignity, and respect
- professional development promotes a focus on student learning consistent with the school vision and goals
- students and staff feel valued and important
- the responsibilities and contributions of each individual are acknowledged
- barriers to student learning are identified, clarified, and addressed
- diversity is considered in developing learning experiences
- lifelong learning is encouraged and modeled
- there is a culture of high expectations for self, student, and staff performance
- technologies are used in teaching and learning
- student and staff accomplishments are recognized and celebrated
- multiple opportunities to learn are available to all students
- the school is organized and aligned for success
- curricular, cocurricular, and extracurricular programs are designed, implemented, evaluated, and refined
- curriculum decisions are based on research, expertise of teachers, and the recommendations of learned societies
- the school culture and climate are assessed on a regular basis
- a variety of sources of information is used to make decisions
- student learning is assessed using a variety of techniques
- multiple sources of information regarding performance are used by staff and students
- a variety of supervisory and evaluation models is employed

- pupil personnel programs are developed to meet the needs of students and their families

ISLLC STANDARD 3

A school administrator is an educational leader who promotes the success of all students by ensuring management of the organization, operations, and resources for a safe, efficient, and effective learning environment.

Knowledge

The administrator has knowledge and understanding of

- theories and models of organizations and the principles of organizational development
- operational procedures at the school and district levels
- principles and issues relating to school safety and security
- human resources management and development
- principles and issues relating to fiscal operations of school management
- principles and issues relating to school facilities and use of space
- legal issues impacting school operations
- current technologies that support management functions

Dispositions

The administrator believes in, values, and is committed to

- making management decisions to enhance learning and teaching
- taking risks to improve schools
- trusting people and their judgments
- accepting responsibilities
- high-quality standards, expectations, and performances
- involving stakeholders in management processes
- a safe environment

Performances

The administrator facilitates processes and engages in activities ensuring that

- knowledge of learning, teaching, and student development is used to inform management decisions
- operational procedures are designed and managed to maximize opportunities for successful learning
- emerging trends are recognized, studied, and applied as appropriate
- operational plans and procedures to achieve the vision and goals of

the school are in place
- collective bargaining and other contractual agreements related to the school are effectively managed
- the school plant, equipment, and support systems operate safely, efficiently, and effectively
- time is managed to maximize attainment of organizational goals
- potential problems and opportunities are identified
- problems are confronted and resolved in a timely manner
- financial, human, and material resources are aligned to the goals of schools
- the school acts entrepreneurially to support continuous improvement
- organizational systems are regularly monitored and modified as needed
- stakeholders are involved in decisions affecting schools
- responsibility is shared to maximize ownership and accountability
- effective problem-framing and problem-solving skills are used
- effective conflict resolution skills are used
- effective group-process and consensus-building skills are used
- effective communication skills are used
- there is effective use of technology to manage school operations
- fiscal resources of the school are managed responsibly, efficiently, and effectively
- a safe, clean, and aesthetically pleasing school environment is created and maintained
- human resource functions support the attainment of school goals
- confidentiality and privacy of school records are maintained

ISLLC STANDARD 4

A school administrator is an educational leader who promotes the success of all students by collaborating with families and community members, responding to diverse community interests and needs, and mobilizing community resources.

Knowledge

The administrator has knowledge and understanding of

- emerging issues and trends that potentially impact the school community
- the conditions and dynamics of the diverse school community
- community resources
- community relations and marketing strategies and processes
- successful models of school, family, business, community, government, and higher-education partnerships

Dispositions

The administrator believes in, values, and is committed to

- schools operating as an integral part of the larger community
- collaboration and communication with families
- involvement of families and other stakeholders in school decision-making processes
- the proposition that diversity enriches the school
- families as partners in the education of their children
- the proposition that families have the best interests of their children in mind
- resources of the family and community needing to be brought to bear on the education of students
- an informed public

Performances

The administrator facilitates processes and engages in activities ensuring that

- high visibility, active involvement, and communication with a larger community is a priority
- relationships with community leaders are identified and nurtured
- information about family and community concerns, expectations, and needs is used regularly
- there is outreach to different business, religious, political, and service agencies and organizations
- credence is given to individuals and groups whose values and opinions may conflict
- the school and community serve one another as resources
- available community resources are secured to help the school solve problems and achieve goals
- partnerships are established with area businesses, institutions of higher education, and community groups to strengthen programs and support school goals
- community youth and family services are integrated with school programs
- community stakeholders are treated equitably
- diversity is recognized and valued
- effective media relations are developed and maintained
- a comprehensive program of community relations is established
- public resources and funds are used appropriately and wisely
- community collaboration is modeled for staff
- opportunities for staff to develop collaborative skills are provided

ISLLC STANDARD 5

A school administrator is an educational leader who promotes the success of all students by acting with integrity, fairness, and in an ethical manner.

Knowledge

The administrator has knowledge and understanding of

- the purpose of education and the role of leadership in modern society
- various ethical frameworks and perspectives on ethics
- the values of the diverse school community
- professional codes of ethics
- the philosophy and history of education

Dispositions

The administrator believes in, values, and is committed to

- the ideal of the common good
- the principles in the Bill of Rights
- the right of every student to a free, quality education
- bringing ethical principles to the decision-making process
- subordinating one's own interest to the good of the school community
- accepting the consequences for upholding one's principles and actions
- using the influence of one's office constructively and productively in the service of all students and their families
- development of a caring school community

Performances

The administrator

- examines personal and professional values
- demonstrates a personal and professional code of ethics
- demonstrates values, beliefs, and attitudes that inspire others to higher levels of performance
- serves as a role model
- accepts responsibility for school operations
- considers the impact of one's administrative practices on others
- uses the influence of the office to enhance the educational program rather than for personal gain
- treats people fairly, equitably, and with dignity and respect
- protects the rights and confidentiality of students and staff
- demonstrates appreciation for and sensitivity to the diversity in the school community

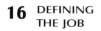
- recognizes and respects the legitimate authority of others
- examines and considers the prevailing values of the diverse school community
- expects that others in the school community will demonstrate integrity and exercise ethical behavior
- opens the school to public scrutiny
- fulfills legal and contractual obligations
- applies laws and procedures fairly, wisely, and considerately

ISLLC STANDARD 6

A school administrator is an educational leader who promotes the success of all students by understanding, responding to, and influencing the larger political, social, economic, legal, and cultural context.

Knowledge

The administrator has knowledge and understanding of

- principles of representative governance that undergird the system of American schools
- the role of public education in developing and renewing a democratic society and an economically productive nation
- the law as related to education and schooling
- the political, social, cultural, and economic systems and processes that impact schools
- models and strategies of change and conflict resolution as applied to the larger political, social, cultural, and economic contexts of schooling
- global issues and forces affecting teaching and learning
- the dynamics of policy development and advocacy under our democratic political system
- the importance of diversity and equity in a democratic society

Dispositions

The administrator believes in, values, and is committed to

- education as a key to opportunity and social mobility
- recognizing a variety of ideas, values, and cultures
- importance of a continuing dialogue with other decision makers affecting education
- actively participating in the political and policy-making context in the service of education
- using legal systems to protect student rights and improve student opportunities

Performances

The administrator facilitates processes and engages in activities ensuring that

- the environment in which schools operate is influenced on behalf of students and their families
- communication occurs among the school community concerning trends, issues, and potential changes in the environment in which schools operate
- there is ongoing dialogue with representatives of diverse community groups
- the school community works within the framework of policies, laws, and regulations enacted by local, state, and federal authorities
- public policy is shaped to provide quality education for students
- lines of communication are developed with decision makers outside the school community

I offer two fundamental reasons for you to adopt and use the *Standards for School Leaders* as your mental framework of the principalship:

1. You can rely on the ISLLC Standards for their breadth and depth. The six areas identified by the Interstate School Leaders Licensure Consortium (ISLLC) competently encompass the basic tasks of the school principal. Thus they provide an authentic "big-picture" perspective of the principal's role.

2. You are likely to encounter the ISLLC Standards in future job-related endeavors. Consider, for example, that 34 states (more than two of every three states in the nation) have adopted the ISLLC Standards as their blueprint for rethinking school leadership. Many of those states are aggressively using the Standards to redefine expectations in areas such as licensure, professional development, and preparation programs (Murphy, 2002). With their expanding influence, the odds increase that you and the Standards will cross paths. Hence the greater your familiarity with the ISLLC Standards, the better you will understand and relate to them. You and those whom you serve and lead will benefit from your increased familiarity with the ISLLC Standards.

RECOMMENDED READINGS RELATED TO "DEFINING THE JOB"

All readings listed below relate to defining and conceptualizing the principal's role. These selections address the essentials of school leadership, such as vision, mission, change, culture, and standards for school leaders.

Peterson and Deal write about analyzing and cultivating a desirable school culture, and Fullan's "culture of change" includes five core competencies that help leaders cope with an increasingly complex and rapidly changing world. Goldring and Rallis offer ways for school principals to embrace and capitalize upon the changes that engulf schools. Hoyle, English, and Steffy synthesize key standards promulgated by various educational leadership groups. Green's book is particularly helpful for interpreting and applying the six ISLCC Standards to the principal's role, and Wilmore's work includes those six plus a section on a seventh Standard applicable for the administrative internship. Sergiovanni's "reflective practice perspective" focuses on issues of diversity, the ISLLC Standards, and a school's character. Kohn challenges our thinking about standards and competition. If you like looking at the "bigger" picture and having your mind stretched a bit, I urge you to examine Thornburg's book on the "new basics in a telematic age." Thornburg analyzes the role of education in the world, not just in the United States, and reviews how that role is dramatically changing because of an exponential explosion of technology.

* * *

Fullan, M. (2001). *Leading in a Culture of Change*. San Francisco: Jossey-Bass.

Goldring, E. B., & Rallis, S. (2000). *Principals of Dynamic Change—Taking Charge of Change*. Thousand Oaks, California: Corwin.

Green, R. L. (2001). *Practicing the Art of Leadership—A Problem-Based Approach to Implementing the ISLLC Standards*. Upper Saddle River, New Jersey: Prentice Hall.

Hoyle, J. R., English, F. W., & Steffy, B. E. (1998). *Skills for Successful 21st-Century School Leaders: Standards for Peak Performers*. Arlington, VA: American Association of School Administrators.

Kohn, A. (2000). *The Schools Our Children Deserve: Moving Beyond Traditional Classrooms and Tougher Standards*. New York: Mariner Books.

Peterson, K. D., & Deal, T. (2002). *The Shaping School Culture Fieldbook*. San Francisco: Jossey-Bass.

Sergiovanni, T. J. (2000). *The Principalship: A Reflective Practice Perspective* (4th ed.). Boston: Allyn & Bacon.

Thornburg, D. (2002). *The New Basics: Education and the Future of Work in the Telematic Age*. Alexandria, VA: The Association for Supervision and Curriculum Development.

Wilmore, E. L. (2002). *Principal Leadership: Applying the New Educational Leadership Constituent Council (ELCC) Standards*. Thousand Oaks, CA: Corwin.

PART II

Doing the Job

An Overview of Tasks Entry-Year Principals Need to Accomplish 4

Part II identifies job-specific knowledge and skills necessary for you to fulfill tasks typically associated with the principalship and specifically focuses on the things that an entry-year principal must accomplish. I have grouped these tasks into three categories:

- Tasks you need to accomplish *before the school year begins*, that is, July and August (see Module 5)
- Tasks you need to accomplish *as the school year begins*, that is, the first day and first week of school (see Module 6)
- Tasks you need to accomplish *as the school year progresses*, that is, each month of the school year (see Module 7)

In an attempt to display the connection between the day-to-day activities of the school principal and the overarching validity of national standards, I correlate the entry-year task list with the ISLLC Standards. As you review the tasks, you will see that I have coded each one according to (1) the ISLLC Standard(s) most closely associated with the task and (2) the level of school organization with which the task is typically associated. The numerals of the different ISLLC standards appear in parentheses following each task. The symbols (E) for Elementary, (M) for Middle and Junior High, and (H) for High school indicate the organizational levels. Please note that some tasks apply to more than one level of school organization and some tasks relate to more than one ISLLC Standard.

As you analyze the list of entry-year principal tasks and their correlation to the ISLLC Standards, you may notice that a preponderance of the tasks are associated with Standard 3, which is the so-called "management standard." Whether we like it or not, the principalship is fraught with management issues. As the principal, you must of course be a leader, but unless you manage successfully, your opportunities to lead will rapidly diminish. Ben Franklin said it well when he observed that, "for want of a nail the shoe was lost; for want of a shoe the horse was lost; and for want of a horse the rider was lost." You may be the greatest educational visionary since John Dewey, but if the lunch line backs up incessantly, if the coffee machine in the teacher's lounge fails to heat, and if textbooks fail to appear because you did not complete the paperwork, be assured that your exemplary leadership skills will take second place to your managerial shortcomings. Say it however you wish, leader-manager or manager-leader, the successful principal must be both.

Furthermore, the earlier you master the managerial tasks associated with the role of the principal, the sooner you can devote more of your time and energy to leadership issues. As you identify and adopt successful strategies to manage the mundane or routine matters, your efficiency increases. Hence your goal should be to get control of your managerial responsibilities so as to decrease the time and energy that you spend on them and increase the amount of attention you give to leadership activities.

The list of tasks for the entry-year principal is extensive and as you review it, you may feel overwhelmed. There are so many things to do. How are you to get it all done? Where do you start? Which things come first? I suggest that you keep the following thoughts in mind as you review the task lists:

- All items on the task list are important; eventually, all of them will need your attention. However, you do not have to accomplish them immediately; you can delay some for a while. As one example, if you assume your position several weeks before the school year begins, you will have several days before you must adopt or announce a method of observing and evaluating teachers. Similarly, there are other tasks on the list that you can delay.

- I listed the items by level of priority. The items at the top of the list take priority over those listed lower down. However, in your situation, local or unique demands may dictate that you address certain items earlier than I have them listed. For example, I listed "review and become familiar with the policy and procedures related to student conduct" near the end of the tasks to be accomplished before the school year begins. If you are assuming a principalship where the school and community is embroiled in a controversy about student discipline, you will find this task leaping to the top of your "Things to do" list. Consult with a mentor or other experienced administrators from your school district to determine if any such idiosyncrasies exist.

- Accomplishing the various tasks efficiently and effectively depends on having accurate and prompt information. As you review each item, think about or make written notes regarding where and how you can quickly acquire relevant and accurate information. Typically, an experienced school secretary is a vital link to formal data (such as the names and telephone numbers of significant community members, performance records of students, and employment records of staff) and informal information (such as the history of a donated gift or why a particular school practice is viewed as "sacred"). In addition, a principal mentor can help you develop a plan to address your tasks in an efficient and effective manner, guide you in gathering data, and introduce you to appropriate contacts.

5 Tasks to Be Accomplished Before the School Year Begins

(JULY–AUGUST)

Become familiar with existing policies and procedures:

(Standard 3) (E) (M) (H)

Locate and read the Board of Education policy manual and the school district's administrative procedures handbook.

Become familiar with the labor-management agreements (master contracts) that exist between the Board of Education and the groups that represent district employees:

(Standard 3) (E) (M) (H)

Read negotiated agreements and identify those articles that pertain to the operation of the school. Among other important information that you need to know, these documents stipulate the procedures, expectations, and timelines that you must observe to complete the evaluation of staff members. Give particular attention to sections that address sick leave, personal leave, and grievance procedures.

MODULE 5: **25**
TASKS TO BE
ACCOMPLISHED
BEFORE THE
SCHOOL YEAR
BEGINS

Become familiar with curriculum (graded courses of study, rubrics, and lists of adopted texts):

(Standard 2) (E) (M) (H)

This topic represents a massive amount of information, which few individuals can comprehend in a short time. As an initial step, learn where these materials are located and analyze how they are organized, so that you can secure them quickly and knowledgeably when the need arises.

Become familiar with the academic performance record of the school and map your leadership strategies accordingly:

(Standard 2) (E) (M) (H)

If the school has a satisfactory performance record, this task will be less critical than if the school has a record of low performance. In the former case, you may need only to review test scores and state or local district report cards, and so forth, and stand ready to assist in maintaining those practices that have produced such performance results. If the school has a low performance record, then the need to develop an improvement plan is more urgent. This complex issue requires the involvement of many school stakeholders and you would be wise to seek the counsel of experienced school administrators. At the very least, you are facing a situation in which you need to conduct an analysis of the test scores and the instructional delivery program, including the appropriateness of the learning goals, instructional materials, and evaluative processes. You must lead others in identifying and implementing the corrective measures needed, securing necessary funding, establishing appropriate timelines, and gathering accurate measurement and assessment data. To reiterate for emphasis, this is a complex issue and I urge you to seek the guidance of more experienced administrators within your district or area.

Review existing handbooks for staff and students:

(Standard 3) (E) (M) (H)

• Verify that the content in the building handbooks is consistent with the policies and procedures outlined in the Board of Education policy manual, the school district's administrative procedures handbook, and the master contracts and agreements that exist between various labor groups and the Board of Education.

• If building-level handbooks are not ready for distribution, determine and complete the necessary preparation.

• Authorize the printing of such building-level handbooks and prepare copies for distribution.

Develop a planned, organized approach to decision making:

(Standard 1) (E) (M) (H)

The "bumper sticker" version of this task admonishes you to "decide how you will decide," which, at first glance, may seem like superfluous advice. However, I recommend that even before you assume the job—or, at the very least, early on in the position—you devote some time to thinking about how you are going to *decide how to decide*. Reflect on how you will identify the issues, how you will develop the alternatives, and how you will choose the proper course of action.

Yes, ultimately, as the building principal, you are responsible for a vast majority of things that happen at the school, and in most cases, you have the authority (and responsibility) to issue the final "say-so." However, just as we encounter the occasional televised warning that viewers should not attempt certain daredevil stunts at home, school leaders should avoid making decisions in isolation. Assuming that you are working with capable people who support the goals of the organization, you enhance your decision-making process when you seek the input and involvement of those persons who have a stake in the decision. In addition, it is more than a matter of inviting others to participate in decision making; school leaders in the 21st century face increasing *demands* that stakeholders be recognized and heard.

> *"Today's principals must practice distributive leadership within a framework of collaboration and shared decision-making. Good principals have always understood the need to work collaboratively rather than in isolation. The challenges of diversity, technology, and accountability often require solutions that are best achieved in concert with others."*

> —(Riggins, 2002)

If you plan to use a participatory decision-making style, then you need to establish and maintain a systematic means of providing opportunities for input and arriving at collaborative decisions. Without some system for collecting and utilizing input, your attempts to operate in a collaborative manner may be reduced to simply conducting polls and announcing results.

Early on in my career as a building administrator, I recognized the value of involving all staff in the operation of the building. After an exposure to the philosophy of participatory management and with the input of staff members, we collaboratively developed and utilized the participatory management procedures that I describe in the following section. These procedures rely on (1) the creation and maintenance of a principal's advisory group and (2) sustaining mutual trust and respect between the administrator and the staff members. The name for the group may vary in different settings. In our case, we called it an "Instructional Improvement Committee" (IIC), and the guidelines we used to conduct its business appear in the following table. (See Table 1.)

MODULE 5: **27**
TASKS TO BE
ACCOMPLISHED
BEFORE THE
SCHOOL YEAR
BEGINS

Table 1

OPERATIONAL GUIDELINES
FOR THE INSTRUCTIONAL IMPROVEMENT COMMITTEE

I. Organization

Members of the IIC shall be equitably chosen representatives of the staff. A representative of the PTO will be invited to attend the IIC on a regular basis to facilitate communication between the staff and the parent group. The principal or her or his designee shall act as the chairperson of the IIC.

II. Purpose

The purpose of the IIC shall be threefold:

A. To act as a screening committee to present and consider alternative solutions to schoolwide concerns.
B. To act as an advisory body to the principal.
C. To act as a communication link to improve organization within the school.

III. Operation

A. Agenda:

(1) Staff members may submit items to the agenda by a) writing the item on the agenda pad provided by the principal in a conspicuous and accessible location and b) signing his or her name as the person submitting the item so that other staff members may know whom to contact for clarification or additional data.

(2) The heading of the IIC agenda pad shall include the following message:

IIC Agenda Pad

To have your item included as a part of the current week's agenda, you must record it on the note pad below by noon of the second weekday that school is in session. Please sign your name so that other staff members may contact you for clarification if desired. Clarify your purpose for submitting the item, that is, "to inform," "to discuss," or "to recommend."

(3) The IIC will consider only properly submitted agenda items, which will subsequently appear on the printed agenda. NOTE: Exceptions to this policy are permissible, if there is consensus among the IIC representatives that particular items may be added to the agenda during the meeting.

(4) The principal shall be responsible for preparing and distributing a written copy of the agenda to all staff members at least 24 hours prior to the meeting so that the IIC members have time to discuss the agenda items with the persons they represent prior to the actual meeting.

---

continued

Table 1 continued

B. <u>Minutes</u>:

Members of the IIC shall designate a recorder at each meeting who shall record the minutes of the meeting and arrange for their reproduction and distribution to all staff members within 48 hours after the meeting. The following is a suggested format and procedure for collecting, recording, and verifying consensus on the action taken, and transmitting the minutes to the entire staff.

Agenda for the Instructional Improvement Committee
Date: _____   Time: _____

1. Identify the chairperson
2. Identify the recorder
3. Identify the timekeeper
4. Establish a timeline for concluding the meeting

NOTE: Before adjourning the meeting, provide time for the recorder to verbally share her or his notes to verify consensus on the description of action taken.

(List agenda items here)

(Record minutes here)

C. <u>Items to Be Considered</u>:

Items considered by the IIC shall be of schoolwide concern. Examples include issues such as grading, curriculum, and allocation of teachers and students.

D. <u>Decision-Making Process</u>:

The use of some problem-solving process is encouraged when appropriate. The IIC shall make decisions through consensus when possible. When consensus cannot be reached and a decision must be made, the IIC may choose either of the following procedures to reach a decision:

(1) The IIC may enter into a formal, structured, problem-solving process.
(2) The IIC may ask the principal to make an administrative decision. Having attended the IIC meetings and listened to the staff input and IIC discussion, the principal is aware of staff concerns and viewpoints and can make a more informed decision.

NOTE: The final responsibility for all decision making rests with the principal.

MODULE 5: **29**
TASKS TO BE
ACCOMPLISHED
BEFORE THE
SCHOOL YEAR
BEGINS

E. Duties of IIC members:

In addition to attending all IIC meetings, members of the IIC shall communicate on a regular basis with the people they represent, discussing agenda items and gathering input prior to the IIC meeting. Following the IIC meeting, the IIC representatives shall inform their constituents of the rationale for actions taken by the IIC.

F. Student Representation:

Representatives of the student body may request that items of interest or concern be placed on the agenda. Such representatives may request or be invited to appear before the IIC regarding the specified interest or concern.

G. Open Meetings:

All meetings of the IIC shall be open to all staff members.

Create and maintain a personal calendar or planner for appointments and commitments:

(Standard 3) (E) (M) (H)

Create, update, and maintain a calendar for the school year:

(Standard 3) (E) (M) (H)

You can enhance the organization and communication of the school by encouraging school stakeholders to submit items to the school calendar, which you then publish and distribute on a regular basis. A variety of computer software programs are available to assist in the creation of a school calendar that you can easily maintain, update, and print for distribution. By keeping notes from one year to the next, you can create a tentative calendar for the upcoming school year, which you can print and distribute to the school stakeholders. Receiving the feedback from stakeholders facilitates planning and helps reduce scheduling conflicts. Including the school calendar in the school's newsletter enhances the school's public relations efforts. I suggest that you consider the following steps in creating and maintaining the school calendar:

- Review the previous year's calendar for events and activities that are likely to recur.

- Inform other staff and community members that you are soliciting items for inclusion on the school calendar.
- Review religious calendars to avoid scheduling school events during religious holidays and celebrations.
- Adopt a means of posting, distributing, and making the calendar available to all stakeholders.
- Adopt a system that assures the opportunity for others to provide ongoing input and review of the school calendar.
- Include events that are specific to the school plus district-level events that affect the school's student body, parents, and staff.

I have listed examples (see Table 2) of events that are typical for a school year and that you will need to schedule, coordinate, and include on a school calendar. The culture (history, traditions, and values) of the school and community in which you work will influence whether certain events occur and the emphasis given to them.

Create and maintain a "next year" folder:

(Standard 3) (E) (M) (H)

- Use this folder to store notes about things that need to be changed or studied but do not require action during the current school year.
- Record some notation in your personal calendar or planner for each event that will remind you to initiate action at an appropriate future date.
- If you are using a participatory management system, allow sufficient time for the input process to occur.

Get acquainted with the physical facility:

(Standard 3) (E) (M) (H)

Conduct a "walk-through" of the building and grounds; familiarize yourself with locks, keys, safety and security systems, lighting, heating and cooling, and water systems. Look for areas that need attention, repair, or maintenance. Develop a checklist of items that you will refer to the custodial or maintenance staff.

Get acquainted with the support staff of the school:

(Standard 3) (Standard 6) (E) (M) (H)

This includes personnel such as the secretary, assistant principal(s), guidance counselor(s), custodian(s), aide(s) or assistant(s), food service workers, school nurse, and so forth. Take advantage of the time that students are not in the building to review expectations and procedures with the building secretary.

MODULE 5: **31**
TASKS TO BE
ACCOMPLISHED
BEFORE THE
SCHOOL YEAR
BEGINS

Table 2

Examples of Events That Are Typical for a School Year		
Level of School Organization	Time of Year	Event
(E) (M) (H)	August	Orientation programs, staff
(E) (M) (H)	August	Orientation programs, students, parents
(E) (M) (H)	All year	Meetings, staff
(E) (M) (H)	All School Yr.	Meetings, school support and governing groups
(E) (M) (H)	All School Yr.	Meetings, student government
(E) (M) (H)	Varies	Assemblies, students
(E) (M) (H)	Varies	Awards and Recognition programs
(H)	Varies	Class rings, order
(M) (H)	Varies	Competition, creative events
(M) (H)	Varies	Competition, athletic events
(M) (H)	Varies	Competition, cheerleading
(M) (H)	Varies	Competition, debate
(M) (H)	Varies	Competition, drill team
(H)	Varies	Dance, formal
(M) (H)	Varies	Dance, informal
(M) (H)	Varies	Exams, final or semester
(E) (M) (H)	Varies	Exhibits, fine arts, science, etc.
(E) (M) (H)	Varies	Fundraising activities, entire school
(E) (M) (H)	Varies	Fundraising activities, special groups
(H)	Varies	Homecoming, social events, elections
(E) (M) (H)	Varies	Identification photos, staff and students
(E) (M) (H)	Varies	Inservice days, staff
(E) (M) (H)	Varies	Intervention sessions, proficiency tests
(E) (M) (H)	Varies	Open House
(E) (M) (H)	Varies	Newsletter, dates for submission of articles
(E) (M) (H)	Varies	Newsletter, dates of publication

continued

Table 2 continued

(E) (M) (H)	Varies	Parent-teacher conferences
(H)	Varies	Parking passes, fee collection
(E) (M) (H)	Varies	Parties, grade level or schoolwide
(E) (M) (H)	Varies	"Pay to participate" fee collection
(E) (M) (H)	Varies	Performances, band
(E) (M) (H)	Varies	Performances, choir or chorus
(E) (M) (H)	Varies	Performances, orchestra
(M) (H)	Varies	Performances, theater, drama
(E) (M) (H)	Varies	Photographs, groups
(E) (M) (H)	Varies	Photographs, special events
(E) (M) (H)	Varies	Photographs, yearbook (staff and students)
(E) (M) (H)	Varies	Proficiency tests
(H)	Varies	Prom, social events, elections
(E) (M) (H)	Varies	School spirit events and activities
(H)	April	Graduation, collection of fees for caps and gowns
(M) (H)	May	Orientation, new students, feeder schools
(H)	June	Graduation, program, speakers
(M) (H)	Summer	Camps, academic and athletic
(E) (M) (H)	Summer	Summer school, enrichment and remedial

Get acquainted with other district administrators, assistants, aides, and secretaries:

(Standard 2) (E) (M) (H)

- Other schools within the district (especially at the same organizational level)
- Central office administrators, that is, Business Department, Food Service Department, Personnel Department, Pupil Services Department, Transportation Department

MODULE 5: **33**
TASKS TO BE
ACCOMPLISHED
BEFORE THE
SCHOOL YEAR
BEGINS

Get acquainted with the public (groups and individuals):

(Standard 6) (E) (M) (H)

- Home-school associations or organizations:

  - These include the parent-teacher organizations or associations. In some communities, these local groups are affiliated with national organizations.
  - Make personal contact with the president of such groups; pledge your involvement and support. Determine how the group functions—the rules and regulations or bylaws.
  - Determine the amount of involvement each group has with the school's monthly newsletter, "coffee with the principal" sessions, and whether the group sponsors any "pet" projects.
  - Determine how the groups function; review handbooks for bylaws, operational procedures, and calendar of events. Identify annual and special projects.
  - Learn the names of standing committees and the committee chairpersons.
  - Determine or develop a schedule of meetings with each group for the school year.

- Parent-advisory groups:

  - These include Steering Committees, Principal-Advisory Councils, Booster Clubs, special interest groups, and so forth.
  - Determine the role of these groups, especially in relation to other existing home-school organizations.
  - Develop a schedule of meetings for the school year.
  - Review handbooks, operational procedures, and so on.

- Media representatives:

  - These include representatives from the local or regional newspaper, radio, and television stations.

Attend district-level administrative sessions related to the new school year:

(Standard 2) (Standard 3) (Standard 6) (E) (M) (H)

Typically, the Superintendent of Schools or her or his designee(s) will conduct these sessions prior to the start of the new school year to convey information and expectations. The following are examples of items usually included in such administrative sessions:

- District goals and areas of special emphasis
- Updated information on legislative and legal matters
- District calendar:

- Board of Education meetings
- District-level administrative meetings
- Principals' meetings by level

Reflect upon district goals and consider their application to or integration with personal goals or goals of subordinates:

(Standard 1) (E) (M) (H)

- Goals for self
- Goals for staff; these include goals that are applicable to all staff members as well as goals that are specific to individual staff members.

Clarify your responsibility for the evaluation of employees:

(Standard 3) (E) (M) (H)

Determine which staff members you are to evaluate. Do not assume that you supervise and evaluate every person who works in the school. In some situations, supervisors other than the principal evaluate teachers in areas such as music, art, physical education, special education, and foreign languages. In addition, there may be teachers who work in more than one building, and you may share responsibility with other administrators for the evaluation of such "traveling" teachers. If you do share evaluation responsibilities with another administrator, contact that person to discuss which one of you will give input to the other, and who will then be responsible for completing the paperwork and conducting the conference.

Issues and tasks that you need to determine for all staff members certified and noncertified or professional and support staff include the following:

- Contractual status (limited or continuing)
- Schedule and deadlines stipulated for observing and evaluating
- Forms required, including signatures of specified parties

Develop an understanding of the district's system for observing and evaluating teachers:

(Standard 2) (Standard 3) (E) (M) (H)

As the principal, you are responsible for the annual evaluation of staff members assigned to you. It is critical that you understand your district's process by which administrators are to formally observe and evaluate teachers. In addition, you will need to know the contract status of the teachers whom you are to observe and evaluate, which is information you can obtain from the Personnel Department. You must also be cognizant of the dates by which you are to complete certain observational and evaluative tasks for different teachers at their various levels of contract status. In other

MODULE 5: **35**
TASKS TO BE
ACCOMPLISHED
BEFORE THE
SCHOOL YEAR
BEGINS

words, you will need to be aware of whom you must observe and when, whom you must evaluate and when, and whom you must conference with and when. This requires an organized approach. To maintain an accurate perspective on the entire evaluation process, I developed and used the chart that appears below (see Table 3). It provides an overview of the types or levels of contract status, such as "limited" or "continuing," and it specifies the various evaluation tasks and their due dates. Contract types, dates, and expectations vary for different districts, so revise your copy accordingly.

Develop and adopt a system for tracking your observation of teachers:

(Standard 2) (Standard 3) (E) (M) (H)

After you have determined which teachers you are to observe, their contract status, and the dates by which you are to observe or evaluate them, you must begin conducting the observations and evaluations.

In order to accomplish this most efficiently, I encourage you to develop some means of organizing and tracking your observation and evaluation of teachers. Using a standard "staff checklist," you can prepare a form for recording due dates for observations, the dates when you actually observed the teachers, and the dates when you met with the teachers to confer and sign the observation/evaluation papers. I developed and used the following system, which I offer as a sample. The number of teacher names listed in each example is limited for illustrative purposes.

Staff Checklist

Name of teacher
Kinch
Schmidt
Strohm
Techman

By adding columns for deadline dates, you create cells in which to enter the dates when you complete the observation or evaluation of each teacher. The contractual status of each employee is reflected by the symbol adjacent to each name on the list. In this example, (L) indicates a teacher on a "limited" contract, (C1) indicates a teacher eligible for a "continuing" contract, and (C2) indicates a teacher who holds a "continuing" contract:

Staff Checklist and Tracking Sheet

	Due Dates		
Name of teacher	11/15	3/15	5/15
Kinch (L)			
Schmidt (C2)			
Strohm (L)			
Techman (C1)			

Table 3

CONTRACT STATUS SHEET (Teacher) _____	Oct. 15	Nov. 15	Mar. 15	May 15
An "X" indicates an item is due on the date listed at the top of each column.				
LIMITED: RENEWAL – 1ST- OR 2ND-YEAR LIMITED OR CONTINUING CONTRACT CONSIDERATION (L1)				
Job targets set and conference conducted	X			
Observation cycle* (1st of 2) completed		X		
Observation cycle* (2nd of 2) completed			X	
Annual Appraisal conference conducted and forms signed				X
CONTINUING: CURRENT YEAR EVALUATION (C1)				
Job targets set and conference conducted	X			
Observation cycle* (1st of 1) completed			X	
Annual appraisal conference conducted and forms signed				X
CONTINUING: CURRENT YEAR EVALUATION (C2)				
Job targets set	X			
Job target conference conducted and forms signed				X

*A generic "observation cycle" typically includes:

(1) Preobservation conference

(2) Observation

(3) Written summary

(4) Postobservation conference and sign-off of forms by the evaluator and the teacher

MODULE 5: **37**
TASKS TO BE
ACCOMPLISHED
BEFORE THE
SCHOOL YEAR
BEGINS

As you conduct observations and conferences, you simply enter the dates in the blank spaces as illustrated below:

Staff Checklist and Tracking Sheet			
	Due Dates		
Name of teacher	*11/15*	*3/15*	*5/15*
Kinch (L)	10/18	2/14	
Schmidt (C2)			4/11
Strohm (L)	10/29	1/26	
Techman (C2)	11/09	2/23	

Develop and adopt a system for observing teachers and instruction:

(Standard 2) (Standard 3) (E) (M) (H)

Determine if your school district prescribes a system for recording and reporting the observation of teachers. If no prescribed system exists, consider the following points as you develop your own style or methodology:

- Comply with the master contract.
- Inform the teachers of the system you will be using to conduct observations and provide rationale for the system you will be using.
- Implement a three-phase process for observing teachers *if* you (1) are committed to helping teachers improve their instructional practices and (2) are adept at managing your time allocation. The three-phase process requires more of your time than does the traditional practice of simply observing the lesson taught and writing a description of what you saw. The three-phase model requires you to:

  - Conduct a preobservation conference with the teacher, mutually determine the instructional goals, and ask the teacher if she or he wants feedback on any particular item(s).
  - Observe the teacher teaching the lesson and record the data sought by the teacher.
  - Conduct a postobservation conference with the teacher, share your observations (data that neutrally describes what you saw), engage the teacher in analyzing and evaluating the data you provide, and establish goals for future teaching.

- Document your observations (names, dates, circumstances). Keep notes of what you observe. Consider the ramifications of recording notes while you observe versus waiting until you leave the observation area. If you and the teacher used a preobservation conference to establish what you will be watching for, the teacher will likely be more comfortable as you take notes during the observation. If the teacher does not understand why you are recording notes during the lesson, he or she may feel uncomfortable and defensive while teaching. However, if you wait until after the lesson to record notes, you may forget some things.

- Share your observations with the teacher as soon after the observation as possible.
- Ask clarifying questions and gather information in the follow-up conference before committing your judgments to writing.
- Keep notes of what was discussed in each conference.

Analyze status of staffing needs:

(Standard 3) (E) (M) (H)

Determine if all positions are filled. If not, decide what action steps are necessary.

Coordinate details with other administrators:

(Standard 3) (E) (M) (H)

- Transportation Department: Become familiar with the bus routes, schedules, and the rules that govern student conduct while being transported. Determine your responsibility for informing the pupils and their parents of such rules.
- Food Service Department: Ascertain the cost of lunches, so that you can include such information in the literature that you provide to the parents and students. Determine the times and procedures related to the lunch service, so that you can integrate and monitor the lunch schedule with the school's master schedule. Notify the Food Service Department of any dates when special events (such as field trips) may influence the daily lunch count.
- Pupil Services Department: Integrate your information with that of this department to account for all students enrolled. Identify students with special needs and verify the provision of services, equipment, materials, and personnel to meet those needs.

Get acquainted with the staff and faculty:

(Standard 2) (Standard 3) (E) (M) (H)

- Determine if you, the superintendent, or her or his designee will write and mail a letter of introduction to all staff members.
- If you write (or can influence the person who writes) the letter of introduction, I suggest that you invite staff members to meet you before the school year begins. You can do this with an informal "drop in and get acquainted before school starts" approach, or you may use a more structured approach with a designated time and place for others to meet you. In some settings, this latter form of "getting acquainted" is sponsored by the district school board or the school's Parent-Teacher Association. If others do not arrange such an

MODULE 5: **39**
TASKS TO BE
ACCOMPLISHED
BEFORE THE
SCHOOL YEAR
BEGINS

event, take the initiative to organize some means of meeting *all* staff members before the first day of school.

- By scheduling such opportunities to get acquainted before the school year begins, you avoid the hectic pace that is certain to descend on you and other staff members once school begins. Making yourself available to *all* staff members demonstrates openness and impartiality that is essential in establishing new relationships; in other words, it helps you avoid giving the impression that your access is limited to a few select staff members. After issuing invitations for all staff members to meet with you, you may also want to schedule meetings with department heads and team leaders to determine their particular concerns, needs, and wants. The earlier you can conduct these "get acquainted" activities, the better; capitalizing on such lead time before the school year begins allows you to collect information pertinent to the school and its personnel, which helps you be better prepared to meet your duties.

Review active purchase orders and verify the presence, or scheduled delivery, of all necessary physical materials:

(Standard 3) (E) (M) (H)

- For faculty and staff: Verify that there are enough teaching manuals, instructional materials, equipment, supplies, furniture, and so on.
- For students: Determine any need for additional textbooks, desks and chairs, and so on.

Analyze the readiness of the building:

(Standard 3) (Standard 4) (E) (M) (H)

- Locate any records or checklists that describe work scheduled for completion during the summer. Determine if any work orders are outstanding. Make certain that repairs requested by staff are completed or that a plan for completion exists.
- Meet with the custodian(s) to assess the school's state of readiness; conduct a "walk-through" of the building with the custodian(s) to survey the readiness of the facility. If it appears that the building will not be ready to open on the date scheduled, immediately contact the superintendent or her or his designee.
- Investigate the preparedness of safety features: alarms and signals for emergency exits, emergency shelter drills, and building lock-downs. Evaluate the presence of posted exit signs and the successful operation of exit doors and areas. Investigate procedures and facilities for the accessibility of handicapped individuals.
- Inspect for cleanliness; survey all floor surfaces, walls, glass, furniture, and grounds.

Analyze the Emergency Crisis Plan:

(Standard 3) (Standard 4) (E) (M) (H)

- Emergency crises include threats, serious injuries, death, and so forth.
- Determine that an emergency plan exists and has been tested and proven workable.
- Verify that staff members are knowledgeable of the plan and are sufficiently trained to implement the plan if the need should arise.

Determine the method for requesting maintenance work:

(Standard 3) (E) (M) (H)

- Determine the process you are to use when communicating a building-level need to the head of the Maintenance Department.
- Discover whether the Maintenance Department head prefers personal notification or the use of a more formal system (or both) when requesting work or materials.
- Also, develop a system that encourages staff members to notify the building office of maintenance needs or safety concerns.

Verify the readiness of all explanatory materials related to the opening of the school year:

(Standard 2) (Standard 3) (E) (M) (H)

Take steps to guarantee the accuracy and professional appearance of all literature distributed to pupils and parents prior to, or on, the first day of school. The list in Table 4 provides examples of items typically included in a parent information packet sent home with the students on the first day of the new school year. Different schools and school years would require slightly different packets of information; however, many of these items should be included each year.

Plan, schedule, and announce the first meeting with the staff and faculty:

(Standard 3) (Standard 1) (E) (M) (H)

Distribute a memo to the staff and faculty with pertinent details, including the agenda for the meeting if it is available.

Plan, schedule, announce or publicize, and conduct orientation sessions for students and parents:

(Standard 2) (Standard 3) (Standard 4) (E) (M) (H)

Consider factors such as the following:

MODULE 5: **41**
TASKS TO BE
ACCOMPLISHED
BEFORE THE
SCHOOL YEAR
BEGINS

Table 4

First Day of School "Parent or Guardian Information Packet"

- Principal's cover letter:
  - Include comments of optimism regarding the new school year.
  - Stress the importance of having the parents or guardians complete and return the attachments that update their student's personal identification and emergency information.
  - Provide any appropriate clarification or information about the student handbook (rules and regulations), fees for school materials, lunches, individual student photographs (date, cost, etc.), and the home-school organization (activities, dues).

- Student Information sheets—for parents to complete and return for the updating of school records
- Emergency Medical Authorization sheet
- Permit for Dispensing Prescription Medication sheet
- Home-School Organization Membership sheet
- Parent Advisory Group Application sheet
- Parent Volunteer sheet
- Student Directory sheet—for voluntary inclusion in PTO fundraiser or directory
- Application for Free or Reduced-Price School Lunch
- Emergency Dismissal Procedure sheet
- School calendar (for the school year, including vacation dates)
- Student handbook
- Program of Studies (high school)

- Which student groups will you accommodate?
- What type of "message" do you want to convey?
- Will you provide a tour of the building, and if so, will you need tour guides?
- Are there appropriate materials for distribution?
- Will other staff members be involved?
- Is there a role for the home-school organization?
- What physical accommodations are needed and are they available? (For example, area in which to meet, seating arrangements, public address system, etc.)

Review and become familiar with the master schedule:

(Standard 3) (E) (M) (H)

Analyze the schedules of each teacher. Confirm the complete and accurate scheduling of *each* student. Confirm that class enrollments are as balanced as possible; classroom assignments (for students and teachers) are accurate; and adequate furniture is in place.

Authorize the printing of class schedules for all teachers and students:

(Standard 3) (E) (M) (H)

After confirming the accuracy of the master schedule (above), implement the process of printing all related schedules.

Authorize the preparation and mailing of appropriate materials to students:

(Standard 3) (Standard 4) (Standard 2) (E) (M) (H)

Typically, these materials include the following:

- A "Welcome to the Building" letter
- An assignment to a teacher-advisor or homeroom teacher
- A copy of the student's daily class schedule
- A notice or confirmation of any special assignments

Review and become familiar with the policies and procedures for individuals or groups to use when requesting the use of the building:

(Standard 3) (Standard 4) (E) (M) (H)

- Become familiar with the district policy on use of school facilities.
- Create and maintain a file of Building Use request forms submitted to you. Maintain a record of the requests that you approve or deny; be sure to date all forms.
- Create a calendar or schedule to maximize the use of the building and avoid scheduling conflicts (see Table 5 for a sample "Building Use Schedule").
- Attempt to collect as many of the requests as possible before finalizing the schedule. This will help you maximize the use of the building.
- If the night custodian(s) is responsible for opening the building to approved groups, provide the custodian(s) with a copy of the approved Building Use Schedule.
- Institute a system to automatically inform the custodian(s) of any revisions made during the school year.

You can expand the Building Use Schedule to include all days of the week and months of the school year as needed. Printing such a form in the landscape format (lengthwise) provides more space for recording notations. There are "user-friendly" computer software programs available that you can use to develop and maintain the schedule of building use at your school.

MODULE 5: **43**
TASKS TO BE
ACCOMPLISHED
BEFORE THE
SCHOOL YEAR
BEGINS

Table 5

	Building Use Schedule										
	ROOM OR FACILITY: Multipurpose Room										
	DAY OF WEEK: Mondays										
	September					October				Etc.	Etc.
	1	8	15	22	29	6	13	20	27		
4:00	Intramural										
4:30	Volleyball (8 weeks)										
5:00	Recreational Center										
5:30											
6:00	Volleyball (12 weeks)										
6:30											
7:00	Rec Center										
7:30											
8:00	"Dancercize" (10 weeks)										
8:30			Men's Basketball – Union								
9:00											
9:30			Bank (16 weeks)								

Review and become familiar with the policy and procedures for securing substitutes when regular employees are absent:

(Standard 3) (E) (M) (H)

Be certain that you know and enforce these policies and procedures and that you communicate any changes to the staff members.

Review and become familiar with the policy and procedures related to student conduct:

(Standard 2) (Standard 3) (Standard 5) (Standard 6) (E) (M) (H)
Generally, you will need to review two basic sources of information:

(1) The Student Code of Conduct as adopted by the Board of Education

(2) The disciplinary policies and procedures used in the building

Keep a copy of the existing student handbook available for quick reference and for recording notations of items that you want to consider changing next year. The Board of Education exercises final approval on the student handbook; you do not have the authority to institute change on your own, but you can, by using appropriate administrative channels, recommend changes.

Experienced principals can attest that discipline and control of students are major concerns of all persons involved with the operation of a school.

Many individuals expect the principal to *solve* disciplinary situations on the assumption that the principal can alter the student's behavior, attitude, and values. You may wish to consider, however, whether you want staff members to automatically involve you in solving all types of disciplinary problems. For example, staff members who are directly involved with a student and her or his instructional or learning program can more promptly and effectively address acts of misconduct that impede the student's academic performance, but fall short of interfering with the rights of others. Teachers decide and control many instructional issues and practices that have a significant influence on student academic performance and behavior. Requiring the person (usually a teacher) who is referring the incident to first assess the type or nature of the misconduct before referring the student to the principal may result in that person choosing a more immediate and effective course of action or remedy. Tables 6 and 7 illustrate two four-part forms that require the reporting person to reflect on the nature of the offense and to consider the two following questions before reporting the incident to the principal:

Question 1: Was the misconduct detrimental to the student *and others*? (See Table 6)

Question 2: Was the misconduct detrimental to the student *only*? (See Table 7)

Review and become familiar with the policy and procedures related to the student-testing program:

(Standard 2) (Standard 3) (E) (M) (H)
Questions to consider regarding issues, topics, and tasks include the following:

MODULE 5: **45**
TASKS TO BE
ACCOMPLISHED
BEFORE THE
SCHOOL YEAR
BEGINS

Table 6

Report of Pupil Misconduct and Subsequent Disciplinary Action
(for acts of misconduct detrimental to *this student and others*)

Name of student: _____

Grade: _____   Advisor/homeroom teacher: _____

Class/activity: _____

Offense: _____

Reported by: _____

  <u>Initial response by person(s) reporting this incident:</u>

  __ 1. Handle in class or activity; submit report only for inclusion in pupil's misconduct file.

  __ 2. Provide emergency time-out at office (detain from __ a.m. / p.m. to __ a.m. / p.m.).

  __ 3. Provide contracted time-out at office (detain from __ a.m. / p.m. to __ a.m. / p.m.).

  __ 4. Refer directly to the principal (only for the following acts):

  __   Possession or use of illegal drugs

  __   Attacking students or staff members (physically, verbally, or in writing)

  __   Extreme cases of defacing property (school or others)

  __   Truancy

  __   Prior agreement between principal and teacher regarding this student

  <u>Follow-up information to clarify the offense (follow-up disciplinary action may include a combination of these items):</u>

  __ 1. Student warned; record notice of warning; no additional consequence

  __ 2. Writing assignment: four-part account (What I did; Why I did it; What I should have done; What I can and will do to not repeat this)

  __ 3. Writing assignment (essay)

  __ 4. Writing assignment (apology)

  __ 5. Isolation (within class or activity)

  __ 6. Restitution (replace or restore)

  __ 7. Restitution (work detail): assigned __ hour(s) to do the following: _____

  __ 8. Restitution (monetary): fined $__ in damages

  __ 9. Detention before school day (requires prior notification of parents)

---

continued

Table 6 (continued)

    __ 10. Detention during noon hour with teacher for __ hours

    __ 11. Detention during noon hour at office (requires principal's approval and scheduling) for __ hour(s)

    __ 12. Detention after school day (requires prior notification of parents)

    __ 13. Parent notified of incident by the student (verified by telephone call witnessed or letter signed and returned by parent)

    __ 14. Parent informed of incident by the reporting teacher

    __ 15. Parent informed of incident by the teacher or advisor

    __ 16. Parent informed of incident by the principal

    __ 17. Discipline form letter or record mailed to the parent; date mailed _____

    __ 18. Emergency removal from school

    __ 19. Law enforcement officials contacted (date contacted) _____

    __ 20. Nurse contacted (date contacted) _____

    __ 21. Conference with pupil and staff; participants: _____

    __ 22. Conference with pupil, parents, and staff; participants: _____

    __ 23. Conference with pupil and staff; participants: _____

    __ 24. Placed on Behavior Contract — copy filed with: _____

    __ 25. Saturday School/date(s) assigned: _____

    __ 26. Suspension In School/date(s) assigned: _____

    __ 27. Suspension Out of School/date(s) assigned: _____

    __ 28. Re-assignment of pupil _____

    __ 29. Reduced school day; terms: _____

    __ 30. Recommend for expulsion _____

Copy Distribution: (While: Advisor) (Yellow: Follow-up to Advisor) (Pink: Office) (Gold: Reporting Person)

- What tests are required?
- What are the laws or regulations that govern the administration of the tests?
- What are the testing dates?
- Who are the students being tested, that is, what grade levels are involved?
- Are there any exempted or excused students?
- Are there any students who require special accommodations such as readers or scribes? Do any students require calculators?
- Are any students granted extra time to complete the tests?
- Where are the tests administered?
- Who will serve as test administrators and proctors?
- Who will train the administrators and proctors?
- When will such training of administrators and proctors occur?
- What are the provisions for test security, storage, distribution, and collection of test materials?

MODULE 5: **47**
TASKS TO BE
ACCOMPLISHED
BEFORE THE
SCHOOL YEAR
BEGINS

Table 7

Report of Pupil Misconduct and Subsequent Disciplinary Action
(for acts of misconduct detrimental to *this student only*)

Name of student: _____

Grade: _____ Advisor or Homeroom Teacher: _____

Offense: _____

Record maintained and reported by: _____

Acts of misconduct:	Dates of occurrence:				
1. Not reporting to class on time					
2. Not bringing necessary materials to class					
3. Too often creating reasons to leave class					
4. Not handing in assignments					
5. Not handing in assignments on time					
6. Demonstrating inattentive behaviors					
7. Bringing distracting items to class					
8. Satisfied with poor, inaccurate work or effort					
9. Rushing to complete in-class assignments					
10. Not proofreading work					
11. Not correcting work when given the chance to do so					
12. Not taking notes during class opportunities					
13. Not participating in teacher-led discussions					
14. Not participating in small-group activities					
15. Slow to begin in-class work or assignments					
16. Not redoing work outside of class					

continued

Table 7 continued

17. Not retaking tests when given chance to do so					
18. Not maintaining an assignment book or record					
19. Not organizing study materials and space					
20. Not seeking help from instructional staff					
21. Seeking help without sufficient personal effort					
22. Other:					
23. Other:					

The frequency of occurrence will influence the teacher's decision when to inform the student's teacher-advisor, guidance counselor, principal, and parent(s) or guardian(s).

<u>Responses to Misconduct Cited Above</u>

Teacher initiated contacts and attempts to correct the situation with the student:

(Date: _____) Action or Result: _____

_____

(Date: _____) Action or Result: _____

_____

Parent informed by: _____ (Date: _____)

Parent informed by: _____ (Date: _____)

Conference conducted: (Date: _____) Participants: _____

_____

Summary of conference: _____

_____

_____

Copy Distribution: (White: Advisor) (Yellow: Follow-up to Advisor)
(Pink: Office) (Gold: Reporting Person)

MODULE 5: **49**
TASKS TO BE
ACCOMPLISHED
BEFORE THE
SCHOOL YEAR
BEGINS

- What are the provisions for returning test materials?
- Are students and parents aware of the testing dates and procedures?
- What are the guidelines regarding student absence and makeup sessions?

Familiarize yourself with existing Special Education services and needs of the building:

(Standard 2) (Standard 3) (E) (M) (H)

Review, or arrange for the review of, all Individualized Education Plans (IEPs) to verify compliance with the special needs addressed in the signed agreements. This includes teachers, aides, supplies, equipment, and types or extent of services provided.

Plan and conduct orientation program for new staff members:

(Standard 3) (Standard 1) (Standard 2) (E) (M) (H)

New staff members are more apt to ask questions in a small-group setting; therefore I recommend that you conduct a "new staff orientation" program *separate from* the first-day meeting with all staff. By providing amenities such as refreshments, nametags, lists of personnel, calendars, and school spirit or pride items, you can foster a positive beginning to the new school year. This group will require detailed instructions regarding school policy and procedures that pertain to their performance of duties. (Note: You need not provide such specificity with the returning, experienced teachers during the first all-staff meeting.)

During the new staff orientation, you will need to do the following:

- Distribute and explain all standard operating materials and procedures (typically the building handbook for teachers includes such items). Allow ample time for the new staff members to review and discuss these materials and ask any questions they might have.

- If a formal teacher-mentoring program exists, verify that all beginning teachers are oriented to it and that all mentor-mentee relationships have been, or will be, initiated. If a formal teacher-mentoring program does not exist, arrange for veteran teachers to assist the beginners.

- Provide an orientation to the building, including a floor plan and tour. If time and transportation permit, offer an orientation to and tour of the school district and surrounding community.

Plan for and conduct the first meeting with the entire staff:

(Standard 3) (Standard 1) (E) (M) (H)

Plan carefully and thoroughly for this session, as it is literally the only opportunity to make a first impression with this group. Do not underestimate the power of a first impression, which with some individuals can truly be a lasting one.

- Decide whether to involve other staff members in the presentation of any information (if so, ask them for their assistance in advance).
- Determine if there is any role for the home-school organization.
- Arrange for the physical accommodations (area in which to meet, seating arrangements, public address system, refreshments, etc.).
- Prior to the meeting, verify the readiness of all materials that you will present and distribute.
- Plan the agenda carefully; be time conscious. Do not address standard operating materials and procedures in as much detail as you did in your meeting with the new staff members. Typically, at the start of the school year, teachers are anxious to attend to their classroom tasks and appreciate a well-organized first-day staff meeting that is limited to information that is new or essential to the opening of school.
- As you build the agenda, consider items and materials such as those listed in the following three tables:
  - Sample Agenda for the First Staff Meeting (see Table 8)
  - Possible Agenda Items for the First Staff Meeting (see Table 9)
  - Checklist of Materials Distributed at the First Staff Meeting (see Table 10)

Table 8

Sample Agenda for the First Staff Meeting

This is a sample agenda for the first staff meeting of the new school year. Different school settings and different school years would necessitate different agendas; however, many of the items listed below represent tasks typically addressed at the start of each school year.

****

Introductions:

Acknowledge staff members, especially new additions.

Collection of personal data:

Provide forms to standardize the collection of addresses, telephone numbers, and so on, for the district and building directories.

Distribution and review of district and building goals

- Emphasize new or special goals as defined by the district office.
- Remind the teachers that they should integrate their annual goals with district and building goals.
- Explain the manner in which teachers are scheduled for annual goal conferences (if it is on a "sign-up" basis, inform the teachers of the procedure for doing so).

MODULE 5: **51**
TASKS TO BE
ACCOMPLISHED
BEFORE THE
SCHOOL YEAR
BEGINS

Review of the staff handbook:

Acknowledge any changes and emphasize legal and personal responsibility topics such as the following:

- Supervision of students, recording and reporting student absence
- Guidelines for modifying student behavior (i.e., disciplinary practices)
- Emergency procedures (i.e., fire drills, civil defense and tornado alerts, earthquakes, civil disturbances, bombs or bomb threats, injured or ill students, procedures for dispensing medication to students, etc.)

Review or preview any new or modified instructional projects or practices related to the following:

- Curriculum and technology (Inform the staff of any programs that will receive special emphasis during the school year.)
- Proficiency tests (Clarify dates of testing, procedures, and so forth.)
- Provisions for students with special needs (Clarify the services staff members must provide for such students; for example, verify that the appropriate staff members understand (1) the features of the Individual Education Plans that apply to the students who qualify for special education programs and (2) the special needs of other students who do not qualify for special education services, but have special conditions that warrant attention, such as health, family, and guardianship issues.)
- Daily assignment books or subject planners for students
- Textbook distribution forms
- Student fee collection forms

Distribute and review information related to students:

- Student handbooks (Acknowledge and explain any changes.)
- Advisory group or homeroom rosters (Ask advisors or homeroom teachers to check with their advisees on the first day of school to verify the accuracy and spelling of student names, addresses, birth dates, parents' names, etc., and to inform the office of any errors.)
- Attendance sheets for each advisory group
- Daily class schedules for advisees
- Class rosters for each teacher

Distribute and review plans for the first day of school with the students:

- Guiding students from their point of arrival to their advisory groups
- Special schedule and activities for the first day of school
- Distribution of, and orientation to, the student handbook and the student daily assignment book

Table 9

<u>Possible Agenda Items for the First Staff Meeting</u>

The following is an alphabetized list of possible topics for the first meeting with the entire staff. You must decide which items warrant inclusion on the agenda for the first staff meeting and which items you will address at another time and in another manner. This also provides a checklist of items for possible inclusion in handbooks for staff, students, and parents.

- Accident forms—staff
- Accident forms—student
- Activity account(s)
- Athletic passes
- Attendance procedures
- Awards—staff, students
- Budget
- Building use—by community, by school groups
- Calendar
- Civil disturbances
- Class lists
- Clinic—procedures
- Commendations
- Computers—policy for use by staff, by students
- Copier use
- Counselors
- Cumulative folders
- Curriculum—updates from summer work
- Custodians
- Directory information
- Discipline—students; guidelines, handbooks
- Emergency Medical Authorization—students
- Emergency procedures— earthquakes, fire drills, power failures, snow, special education, threats against staff and students, tornados

- Enrollment—staff, health insurance
- Enrollment—students
- Evaluation—instructional program; staff, student
- Fees—student
- Field trips
- Financial aid—students
- Fundraising activities
- Furniture needs
- Goals—district, building, individual
- Grading policy
- Handbook—staff, students, parents
- Illness—personal, students
- Instructional Materials Center and library— procedures, new materials
- Insurance forms—staff, students
- Intervention—plans, teams
- Keys—building, rooms, storage areas
- Lesson plans—books, policy
- Lockers—locks, assignments
- Lunch—staff, student, menus, procedures, schedules
- Maintenance—requests
- Medication—students, procedures

MODULE 5: **53**
TASKS TO BE
ACCOMPLISHED
BEFORE THE
SCHOOL YEAR
BEGINS

- Meetings—faculty, department, team, grade level
- Newsletter
- Office procedures
- Open House—date(s), policy, procedures
- Paper supply
- Parent-teacher conferences—dates, procedures
- Parent-teacher organization—meetings, membership
- Parking of automobiles—permits, tags
- Payroll—dates, procedures
- Pictures—staff, students, dates
- Professional growth activities
- Proficiency tests—dates, procedures
- Public address system—policy, use of
- Purchase orders
- Recess—duty, procedures, schedule
- Recycling—procedure
- Recognition programs—staff, students
- Renovations—buildings, grounds
- Repair requests
- Security—procedures
- Sign-in—procedures
- Special Education
- Student teachers
- Substitute principal—policy
- Substitute teachers—policy for securing; lesson plans
- Suspension—students
- Supplemental contracts
- Technology—updates
- Telephone usage policy
- Textbooks—distribution, record forms
- Volunteers

Table 10

Checklist of Materials Distributed at the First Staff Meeting

The following section provides a generic checklist of materials that are distributed to teachers at the start of the school year. The inclusion of particular items will vary according to the organizational level of the school (elementary, middle, or high school).

COPIES OF THE AGENDA

HANDBOOKS:
__ District
__ Building

DUTY ASSIGNMENTS

continued

Table 10 continued

INSTRUCTIONAL MATERIALS:
___ Lesson plan books
___ Grade books (paper or computer systems)
___ Teacher manuals for subject areas

ATTENDANCE—STUDENT:
___ Rosters:
___ Advisory group or homeroom
___ Instructional classes
___ Materials for students:
___ Class schedules
___ Insurance forms
___ Forms:
___ To report student absence
___ To report early dismissal
___ To report student tardiness
___ To report student enrollment
___ To report student withdrawal
___ To have students report to the office
___ To collect demographic information from students
___ Student Passes

MISCONDUCT—STUDENT:
___ Discipline notices (to students, parents, office, other staff
      members)
___ Discipline reports
___ Office referrals

ACADEMIC STATUS—STUDENTS:
___ Progress reports (midterm)
___ Progress reports (end of term)
___ Eligibility reports
___ Forms for reporting student academic progress

MISCELLANEOUS:
___ Forms:
___ Bus Transportation Request
___ Certificated Staff Member Absence
___ Class Coverage
___ Dental and Medical Claim
___ Emergency Medical Authorization (student)

MODULE 5: **55**
TASKS TO BE
ACCOMPLISHED
BEFORE THE
SCHOOL YEAR
BEGINS

___ Field Trip Request

___ Field Trip Evaluation

___ Personal Leave Request

___ Request for Attendance at Professional Meeting

___ Request for Mediation

___ Request for Supplies

___ "Student of the Week or Month" Nomination

___ Work Request (Custodial—Maintenance)

___ Intercom instructions

___ Long-distance telephone log

___ Long-distance telephone user information

___ Recycling information

6 Tasks to Be Accomplished as the School Year Begins

(The First Day of School)

The first day of school is a special day; it is a kind of annual "rite of passage." For most persons associated with the school—the students and their family members, the building staff, central office personnel, and members of the Board of Education—the first day of school is a significant day. Consequently, it is a significant day for the school principal—especially if the principal is a novice. The following list identifies many of the tasks that the building leader must address on the all-important first day of the new school year.

Supervise or monitor the *total* operation:

(Standard 3) (E) (M) (H)
Anticipate issues and tasks related, but not limited, to the following:

- Your arrival at the building; be early to assure that you are ready and organized, confirm with the custodian(s) that the physical facility is operational, and consult with the support staff (assistant principal, guidance counselor, building secretary) regarding any logistics that need last-minute attention.
- Last-minute announcements to the staff. (Depending on the size of the school and number of staff members, you may relay this information by printed message, public address announcements, or by a brief "huddle" staff meeting.) Remind staff members of the first-day schedule, which will probably vary from the regular daily schedule

MODULE 6: **57**
TASKS TO BE
ACCOMPLISHED
AS THE SCHOOL
YEAR BEGINS
(THE FIRST DAY)

- Posting of advisory group or homeroom lists.
- Arrival of students. (Anticipate some late buses and expect a larger-than-usual number of parents bringing their students to the school.)
- Anticipate the appearance of some students who are not officially enrolled; be prepared to accommodate the enrollment of such students.
- Assignment and routing of students to the proper areas (advisory or homeroom or other assembly area).
- Supervision of students' arrival; assure safety and positive reception of the students.
- Public address or televised greeting to students.
- Visibility to staff and students. (Walk about the building, visit classrooms, be introduced or introduce self to students.)
- Enrollment and attendance. (Have teachers verify and report data to the building office; principal or designee to relay figures to the district office.)
- Emergency procedures; fire drills, emergency shelter drills, and so forth. (Verify that teachers review these with students and verify that appropriate signs are posted.)
- Clinic or nurse's office. (Verify that students are advised of location and procedures.)
- Lunch hour: Supervision of cafeteria and recess or activities; have alternate plans ready for inside recess days. Several hours before the lunch line is to open, greet the cafeteria staff; confirm readiness, service times and procedures. During the hours of service, supervise or delegate appropriate supervision to facilitate efficient operation of the lunchroom. (Note: If the school provides a breakfast program for students, consult with the cafeteria staff earlier in the day.)
- Dismissal plans and procedures:

  - Are students aware of their bus assignments to return home?
  - Do students return to their advisory groups or homerooms or leave from their last-period class?
  - Distribution of information for parents—"First day of school parent information packet" delivered by students to their parent(s) or guardian(s)
  - Dismissal of students (anticipate some late buses)
  - Supervision of students at dismissal

- Feedback from staff regarding problems or issues that need attention or correction; depending on the size of the school, this may be achieved via a quick staff meeting or "huddle" to ask, "How did things go?" You may choose to collect feedback via written notes submitted by staff members to you or a delegated person.
- "Phone duty": When students are unhappy, parents are unhappy, and this cycle is accelerated on the first day of school. You may receive calls of disgruntlement throughout the day, if students in your school have access to their parents (i.e., pay phones or cell phones). Typically,

you can expect most of the calls from parents after the students arrive at their homes. Be prepared to receive requests from parents to have their children reassigned to a preferred teacher-advisor, family team, foreign language class, subject teacher, subject area section, or level of instruction. The level of instruction will usually be an issue in any subject area where achievement grouping is used. Be aware that if you approve a parental request to change a student's level of instruction, you will probably "override" a recommendation made by a teacher or team of teachers. I suggest that you consult with the teacher(s) and/or counselor(s) *before* you approve any parental requests. In all such telephone conversations, demonstrate a willingness to listen; express a commitment to investigate; promise that you, or someone more familiar to the situation, will report to the caller within a specified period; and make a note to verify at some point in the future that you or your designee returned the call as promised.

Tasks to Be 7 Accomplished as the School Year Progresses

(EACH WEEK)

Some tasks routinely require your attention each week; the following list identifies such items. While this list is short in appearance, the time required to complete each item is lengthy. However, with experience, your efficiency for accomplishing these tasks will increase.

Review your job-related goals and progress toward accomplishing them, subtasks related to accomplishing them, and the associated time frame:

(Depending on the nature of your chosen goals, this task may relate to all six ISLLC Standards) (E) (M) (H)

Review progress achieved toward conducting observation of teachers and the completion of required paperwork:

(Standard 2) (Standard 3) (E) (M) (H)

Review and revise the "Special Events Calendar":

(Standard 3) (Standard 4) (E) (M) (H)

Review, revise, and update the schedule for substitute teachers:

(Standard 3) (Standard 2) (E) (M) (H)

Conduct a "walk-through" of the building and grounds to review the condition of the physical facilities:

(Standard 3) (E) (M) (H)

Tasks to Be Accomplished as the School Year Progresses 8

(EACH MONTH)

In addition to the weekly tasks identified in the previous module, there are tasks that routinely require your attention each month. Here again, with experience, your efficiency in accomplishing these tasks will increase.

Conduct emergency safety drills as required by law:

(Standard 3) (E) (M) (H)

Laws vary from state to state. Be cognizant of and responsive to laws applicable to your location that specify your responsibility to conduct various emergency safety drills. Examples of such drills include fire, tornado, emergency shelter, and public emergency ("lockdown"). Typically, the laws address items such as the type of drill, the frequency of the drill, and provisions for keeping doors and exits unlocked while school is in session and when the buildings are otherwise open to the public. The laws usually require that a log of such drills be maintained and available for inspection upon request.

Attend district-level administrative meetings and district-level principals' meetings as required (usually a minimum of one meeting per group per month):

(Standard 3) (E) (M) (H)

Conduct building-level meetings (total staff, units, and departments):

(Standard 3) (Standard 2) (Standard 1) (E) (M) (H)

You can enhance internal communication and operational efficiency by promptly sharing information from the central office with staff members in the building. Some of this information may be communicated in written form, thus reducing the need to bring staff members together for a meeting. However, some information is better delivered with the personal touch: a face-to-face meeting. Conduct these sessions as immediately as possible after you receive such information. The frequency of these meetings will depend on the frequency of the central office meetings and communiqués received.

Develop and distribute altered class schedules to the teachers for those dates when special events will change or disrupt the regular daily class schedules:

(Standard 3) (E) (M) (H)

Examples include special performance groups and individuals and student rallies. Coordinate this task with the "Special Events Calendar." Maintain a record of classes shortened or cancelled, so that you can decide which classes to shorten or cancel on an informed and equitable basis.

Monitor and manage the publication of a school newsletter:

(Standard 4) (Standard 6) (Standard 1) (Standard 3) (E) (M) (H)

Assure the regular distribution of a school-based publication that is professional in appearance (error proof), easy to read, positive in its tenor, and informative. Consider input from staff, students, parents, and community. From this publication, the public will typically form impressions of the school, the school district, and its employees.

Conduct public relations "outreach" programs (not necessarily each month):

(Standard 4) (E) (M) (H)

Examples include "Coffee with the Principal," "Grandparents' Day at School," "Donuts with Dad," and "Muffins with Mom."

Attend meeting of the parent-school group (typically scheduled each month):

(Standard 1) (Standard 4) (E) (M) (H)

MODULE 8: **63**
TASKS TO BE
ACCOMPLISHED AS
THE SCHOOL YEAR
PROGRESSES
(EACH MONTH)

Attend meeting of the parent-advisory group (not necessarily scheduled each month):

(Standard 4) (Standard 3) (Standard 6) (E) (M) (H)

Review dates and tasks associated with the Proficiency tests:

(Standard 3) (Standard 2) (E) (M) (H)

9 Tasks to Be Accomplished as the School Year Progresses

(SEPTEMBER)

Review the list of tasks that are typically performed each week and each month:

(Standard 3) (E) (M) (H)

These lists appear in Modules 7 and 8, respectively.

Schedule principal-teacher goal conferences:

(Standard 2) (Standard 3) (E) (M) (H)

If you want to accommodate teachers' preferences for dates and times to confer, you can convert and post a teacher checklist as a sign-up sheet.

Conduct principal-teacher job goal conferences (as required to satisfy the deadlines stipulated by the master contract):

(Standard 2) (Standard 3) (E) (M) (H)

Confirm (with the staff) the format of any "parent visitation nights," that is, "Open Houses":

(Standard 3) (Standard 4) (E) (M) (H)

MODULE 9: **65**
TASKS TO BE
ACCOMPLISHED AS
THE SCHOOL YEAR
PROGRESSES
(SEPTEMBER)

**Announce to or inform the public
of details related to any "parent
visitation nights," that is, "Open Houses":**

(Standard 3) (Standard 4) (E) (M) (H)

**Prepare for the first meeting
with the parent-school organization:**

(Standard 4) (E) (M) (H)

**Prepare for the first meeting
with the parent-advisory group:**

(Standard 4) (Standard 3) (Standard 6) (E) (M) (H)

**Initiate and announce
plans for school committees:**

(Standard 1) (Standard 2) (Standard 3) (E) (M) (H)

**Review plans for assuring the
presence and maintenance of a
student-government organization
based on the principles of democracy:**

(Standard 2) (Standard 3) (E) (M) (H)

Issues include the identification of capable staff sponsor(s), democratic election process, calendar of activities, and so forth.

**Create a plan and schedule for
observing teachers as required
by the formal evaluation process:**

(Standard 2) (Standard 3) (E) (M) (H)

**Identify and meet with those teachers
or sponsors of student performance
groups to establish and clarify
details related to said performances:**

(Standard 1) (Standard 2) (Standard 3) (Standard 4) (Standard 5) (Standard 6) (E) (M) (H)

Issues include:

- Dates
- Hours
- Length of program

- Expenses
- Location of program—on or off campus
- Transportation, if performing off campus
- Approval for travel, if off campus
- Special effects, equipment
- Parental awareness—permission for students to attend special rehearsals or travel

Initiate plans for the school yearbook:

(Standard 4) (Standard 3) (E) (M) (H)

Confirm or recruit a sponsor, determine expenses, and review guidelines regarding groups and activities that are or are not included in the yearbook.

Tasks to Be Accomplished as the School Year Progresses 10

(OCTOBER)

Review the list of tasks that are typically performed each week and each month:

(Standard 3) (E) (M) (H)
These lists appear in Modules 7 and 8, respectively.

Conduct inservice training sessions with those staff members who will proctor the fall Proficiency tests:

(Standard 2) (Standard 3) (E) (M) (H)

Conduct and document formal observations of and conferences with staff members (as required to satisfy the deadlines stipulated by the master contract):

(Standard 2) (Standard 3) (E) (M) (H)
Develop and maintain a record-keeping system to meet your supervisory and evaluative responsibilities with *both* certified and noncertified employees.

Perform tasks related to
the reporting of pupil progress:

(Standard 2) (Standard 3) (E) (M) (H)

Determine how information for pupil progress reports is gathered, reported, and recorded. Verify that the necessary forms are available. Establish and communicate the essential deadlines.

Develop and maintain a system that
informs parents or guardians
each term, if their child has exceeded
the acceptable number of absences:

(Standard 3) (Standard 2) (Standard 1) (E) (M) (H)

Inform the parents or guardians of the ramifications of such excessive absences. District policy will dictate the ramifications; these may be tempered by whether a student's absence is excused or unexcused. Unexcused absences may result in a reduction of letter grades, loss of credit, or retention at a grade level.

Develop and maintain a system that
informs any student who is 18 years of
age or older each term if the student has
exceeded the acceptable number of absences:

(Standard 3) (Standard 2) (Standard 1) (H)

Inform the student of legal age of the ramifications of excessive absences.

If parent-teacher conferences are part
of the system for reporting pupil progress,
offer assistance to teachers in their preparation
for and their conducting of such conferences:

(Standard 2) (Standard 1) (Standard 3) (E) (M) (H)

Such assistance is particularly important for inexperienced teachers. Consider providing print material and role-playing experiences for beginning teachers as they prepare to conduct the conferences. Numerous professional organizations have created resources that you can collect and distribute to address topics such as the following:

- Scheduling and planning for parent-teacher conferences
- Choosing conference topics and student materials
- Communicating with the parents
- Conducting the conference
- Closing the conference

An equally important issue is to decide if the student will participate in the conference.

MODULE 10: **69**
TASKS TO BE
ACCOMPLISHED AS
THE SCHOOL YEAR
PROGRESSES
(OCTOBER)

Administer fall Proficiency test:

(Standard 3) (Standard 2) (E) (M) (H)

Conduct makeup sessions for fall Proficiency test:

(Standard 3) (Standard 2) (E) (M) (H)

11 Tasks to Be Accomplished as the School Year Progresses

(NOVEMBER)

Review the list of tasks that are typically performed each week and each month:

(Standard 3) (E) (M) (H)
These lists appear in Modules 7 and 8, respectively.

Conduct and document formal observations of and conferences with staff members (as required to satisfy the deadlines stipulated by the master contract):

(Standard 2) (Standard 3) (E) (M) (H)
Develop and maintain a record-keeping system to meet your supervisory and evaluative responsibilities with *both* certified and noncertified employees.

Review and monitor the intervention phase of instruction:

(Standard 2) (E) (M) (H)

- Involve teachers in the identification of students who are not responding to regular instructional techniques and need special intervention strategies.
- Facilitate the teacher's discussion and selection of appropriate strategies for such students.

MODULE 11: **71**
TASKS TO BE
ACCOMPLISHED
AS THE SCHOOL
YEAR PROGRESSES
(NOVEMBER)

- Develop a system to monitor the teacher's and team's provision of the intervention strategies that were chosen.

Conduct makeup sessions for fall Proficiency test:

(Standard 3) (Standard 2) (E) (M) (H)

Monitor the academic progress of any pupils who were reassigned in response to parental requests:

(Standard 2) (E) (M) (H)

12 Tasks to Be Accomplished as the School Year Progresses

(DECEMBER)

Review the list of tasks that are typically performed each week and each month:

(Standard 3) (E) (M) (H)

These lists appear in Modules 7 and 8, respectively.

Conduct and document formal observations of and conferences with staff members (as required to satisfy the deadlines stipulated by the master contract):

(Standard 2) (Standard 3) (E) (M) (H)

Develop and maintain a record-keeping system to meet your supervisory and evaluative responsibilities with *both* certified and noncertified employees.

Perform tasks related to the reporting of pupil progress:

(Standard 2) (Standard 3) (E) (M) (H)

- Verify that the necessary forms are available and that staff members are familiar with the procedures for completing those forms.
- Remind staff members of the deadlines.

MODULE 12: **73**
TASKS TO BE
ACCOMPLISHED
AS THE SCHOOL
YEAR PROGRESSES
(DECEMBER)

Monitor the system that informs parents or guardians each term if their child has exceeded the limits of the acceptable number of absences:

(Standard 3) (Standard 2) (Standard 1) (E) (M) (H)

Also, communicate the ramifications of such excessive absence.

Prepare for any midyear award and recognition programs for students:

(Standard 2) (Standard 4) (Standard 3) (E) (M) (H)

- Review award categories.
- Review qualification standards.
- Announce to and remind staff of pertinent details including the categories and standards.
- Identify recipients. (Provide means for teachers and sponsors to submit names.)
- Confirm sufficient inventory of awards to be presented (if they are to be supplied by the administration).
- Identify person(s) who will present the awards and recognition.
- Based on the number of awards to be presented, calculate the length (time) of the awards assembly, and develop and announce the schedule, including any changes to be made to the regular class schedule.

Ascertain the district's time frame for submitting appropriation and budgetary requests for the next school year:

(Standard 3) (Standard 2) (Standard 1) (E) (M) (H)

If the district's time frame for submitting appropriation and budgetary requests for the next school year applies to this month, involve staff in identifying needs:

(Standard 3) (Standard 2) (Standard 1) (E) (M) (H)

This includes paper orders, plan books, grade books, glue, textbooks, and so forth.

Identify procedures related to submitting budgetary requests for the next school year:

(Standard 3) (Standard 2) (Standard 1) (E) (M) (H)

To determine budgetary needs, consider factors such as the following:

- Anticipated student enrollment
- Age, condition of existing materials
- Curricular developments (Are any new programs and materials being implemented?)

In addition, you will need to perform the following tasks:

- Project the probable amount of available funds—district budget, principal's account, donated funds (home-school group?).
- Determine the deadline for all purchase orders to be delivered to the central office.
- Establish and inform staff of the procedure for determining the allocation of funds (i.e., who decides how much money is given to whom? Will staff members be involved? Are there criteria for allocating funds?).
- Estimate and inform staff of the time frame for submitting requests for funds.
- Determine availability of and provide all necessary forms.
- Distribute any forms related to staff requests for donated funds.

Tasks to Be Accomplished as the School Year Progresses 13

(JANUARY)

Review the list of tasks that are typically performed each week and each month:

(Standard 3) (E) (M) (H)
These lists appear in Modules 7 and 8, respectively.

Conduct and document formal observations of and conferences with staff members (as required to satisfy time stipulations within the master contract):

(Standard 2) (Standard 3) (E) (M) (H)
Maintain a record-keeping system to meet your supervisory and evaluative responsibilities with *both* certified and noncertified employees.

Conduct inservice training sessions with those staff members who will proctor the Proficiency tests:

(Standard 3) (Standard 2) (E) (M) (H)

Perform tasks related to the reporting of pupil progress:

(Standard 2) (Standard 3) (E) (M) (H)

- Verify that the necessary forms are available.
- Establish and communicate the essential deadlines.

Conduct midyear award and recognition programs for students:

(Standard 2) (Standard 4) (Standard 3) (E) (M) (H)

Identify any senior who has the potential to not meet the requirements for graduation:

(Standard 3) (Standard 2) (Standard 5) (H)

Verify legal notification of the following individuals if a student may not graduate:

- The parents of any such student under eighteen years of age
- The student, if eighteen years of age or older

Ascertain the district's time frame for submitting appropriation and budgetary requests for the next school year:

(Standard 3) (Standard 2) (Standard 1) (E) (M) (H)

If the district's time frame for submitting appropriation and budgetary requests for the next school year applies to this month, involve staff in identifying needs:

(Standard 3) (Standard 2) (Standard 1) (E) (M) (H)

This includes paper orders, plan books, grade books, glue, textbooks, and so forth.

Identify procedures related to submitting budgetary requests for the next school year:

(Standard 3) (Standard 2) (Standard 1) (E) (M) (H)

To determine budgetary needs, consider factors such as the following:

- Age, condition of existing materials
- Anticipated student enrollment
- Curricular developments (Are any new programs and materials being implemented?)

In addition, you will need to perform the following tasks:

- Project the probable amount of available funds—district budget, principal's account, donated funds (home-school group?).
- Determine the deadline for all purchase orders to be delivered to the central office.

MODULE 13: **77**
TASKS TO BE
ACCOMPLISHED
AS THE
SCHOOL YEAR
PROGRESSES

- Establish and inform staff of the procedure for determining the allocation of funds (i.e., who decides how much money is given to whom? Will staff members be involved? Are there criteria for allocating funds?).
- Estimate and inform staff of the time frame for submitting requests for funds.
- Determine availability of and provide all necessary forms.
- Distribute any forms related to staff requests for donated funds.

14 Tasks to Be Accomplished as the School Year Progresses

(FEBRUARY)

Review the list of tasks that are typically performed each week and each month:

> (Standard 3) (E) (M) (H)
> These lists appear in Modules 7 and 8, respectively.

Conduct and document formal observations of and conferences with staff members (as required to satisfy time stipulations within the master contract):

> (Standard 2) (Standard 3) (E) (M) (H)
> Maintain a record-keeping system to meet your supervisory and evaluative responsibilities with *both* certified and noncertified employees.

Conduct inservice training sessions with those staff members who will proctor the Proficiency tests:

> (Standard 3) (Standard 2) (E) (M) (H)

Administer Proficiency tests:

> (Standard 3) (Standard 2) (E) (M) (H)

Conduct makeup sessions for Proficiency tests:

> (Standard 3) (Standard 2) (E) (M) (H)

MODULE 14: **79**
TASKS TO BE
ACCOMPLISHED
AS THE
SCHOOL YEAR
PROGRESSES
(FEBRUARY)

Begin the process of identifying students for possible retention:

(Standard 2) (E) (M) (H)

Begin the process of identifying and selecting recipient(s) for any end-of-year employee recognition awards and programs:

(Standard 2) (Standard 4) (E) (M) (H)

If this process involves the participation of other people, allow sufficient time for the process to occur.

Ascertain the district's time frame for submitting appropriation and budgetary requests for the next school year:

(Standard 3) (Standard 2) (Standard 1) (E) (M) (H)

If the district's time frame for submitting appropriation and budgetary requests for the next school year applies to this month, involve staff in identifying needs:

(Standard 3) (Standard 2) (Standard 1) (E) (M) (H)

This includes paper orders, plan books, grade books, glue, textbooks, and so forth.

Identify procedures related to submitting budgetary requests for the next school year:

(Standard 3) (Standard 2) (Standard 1) (E) (M) (H)

To determine budgetary needs, consider factors such as the following:

- Age, condition of existing materials
- Anticipated student enrollment
- Curricular developments (Are any new programs and materials being implemented?)

In addition, you will need to perform the following tasks:

- Project the probable amount of available funds—district budget, principal's account, donated funds (home-school group?).
- Determine the deadline for all purchase orders to be delivered to the central office.
- Establish and inform staff of the procedure for determining the allocation of funds (i.e., who decides how much money is given to whom? Will staff members be involved? Are there criteria for allocating funds?).
- Estimate and inform staff of the time frame for submitting requests for funds.
- Determine availability of and provide all necessary forms.
- Distribute any forms related to staff requests for donated funds.

15 Tasks to Be Accomplished as the School Year Progresses

(MARCH)

Review the list of tasks that are typically performed each week and each month:

(Standard 3) (E) (M) (H)
These lists appear in Modules 7 and 8, respectively.

Conduct and document formal observations and conferences with staff members (as required to satisfy time stipulations within the master contract):

(Standard 2) (Standard 3) (E) (M) (H)
Maintain a record-keeping system to meet your supervisory and evaluative responsibilities with *both* certified and noncertified employees.

Ascertain the district's time frame for submitting appropriation and budgetary requests for the next school year:

(Standard 3) (Standard 2) (Standard 1) (E) (M) (H)

MODULE 15: **81**
TASKS TO BE
ACCOMPLISHED
AS THE
SCHOOL YEAR
PROGRESSES
(MARCH)

If the district's time frame for submitting appropriation and budgetary requests for the next school year applies to this month, involve staff in identifying needs:

(Standard 3) (Standard 2) (Standard 1) (E) (M) (H)

This includes paper orders, plan books, grade books, glue, textbooks, and so forth.

Identify procedures related to submitting budgetary requests for the next school year:

(Standard 3) (Standard 2) (Standard 1) (E) (M) (H)

To determine budgetary needs, consider factors such as the following:

- Age, condition of existing materials
- Anticipated student enrollment
- Curricular developments (Are any new programs and materials being implemented?)

In addition, you will need to perform the following tasks:

- Project the probable amount of available funds—district budget, principal's account, donated funds (home-school group?).
- Determine the deadline for all purchase orders to be delivered to the central office.
- Establish and inform staff of the procedure for determining the allocation of funds (i.e., who decides how much money is given to whom? Will staff members be involved? Are there criteria for allocating funds?).
- Estimate and inform staff of the time frame for submitting requests for funds.
- Determine availability of and provide all necessary forms.
- Distribute any forms related to staff requests for donated funds.

Review and implement appropriate action steps related to the "End-of-School-Year Checklist for the Principal":

(Standard 3) (E) (M) (H)

A sample "End-of-School-Year Checklist for the Principal" is available in Table 11.

Administer the state Proficiency tests:

(Standard 2) (Standard 3) (E) (M) (H)

Table 11

<hr>

<u>End-of-School-Year Checklist for the Principal</u>

__ 1. Provide sufficient lead time so that staff members can give input to the master schedule for the next school year.

__ 2. Establish and announce the master schedule for the next school year.

__ 3. Identify employment vacancies and positions that will need to be filled for the next school year.

__ 4. Initiate and implement steps to recruit replacements for vacant employment positions.

__ 5. Initiate and implement steps related to the budgetary process for the next school year.

__ 6. Verify the accuracy of records and notations related to any students retained at their present grade level.

__ 7. Coordinate the transfer of student records and related materials to other schools.

__ 8. Inform faculty of procedures related to the reporting and recording of final progress reports for students.

__ 9. Collect information regarding any unpaid fees; announce and implement policies related to unpaid fees (i.e., were grade reports to parents withheld? Were students and parents notified?).

__ 10. Implement procedures to collect textbooks from students.

__ 11. Implement procedures related to the inventory of supplies, materials, equipment, and so on.

__ 12. Implement procedure for students to remove items from desks and lockers.

__ 13. Review needs of the physical plant and the school grounds in preparation for requesting summer repairs and maintenance.

__ 14. Review plans and calendar for summer cleaning by building custodian(s).

__ 15. Prepare and distribute memo for staff members that clarifies duties to be performed before they leave for the summer (see sample in Table 12).

Conduct makeup sessions for Proficiency test:

(Standard 3) (Standard 2) (E) (M) (H)

Plan for and conduct "kindergarten round-up":

(Standard 3) (E)

MODULE 15: **83**
TASKS TO BE
ACCOMPLISHED
AS THE
SCHOOL YEAR
PROGRESSES
(MARCH)

- Design new or review existing methods for registering children who are eligible to attend kindergarten.
- Arrange for the involvement of appropriate screening personnel, consistent with local and state laws or regulations.
- Design new or review existing methods for informing and encouraging parents of children eligible for kindergarten to initiate the registration process.

Begin preparations for summer school programs:

(Standard 2) (Standard 3) (E) (M) (H)

Be prepared to submit recommendations for contract renewals to the appropriate Central Office administrator:

(Standard 2) (Standard 3) (E) (M) (H)

Begin or continue the process of identifying students for possible retention:

(Standard 2) (E) (M) (H)

Typically, parents want to be informed that their child is a candidate for retention with sufficient advance notice that they can assist their child in efforts to avoid the retention (of course there are exceptions, as some parents are in agreement with the retention). However, school personnel must avoid informing the parents of the probability of retention so early in the school year that parents infer that the teachers are predisposed to the inevitability of the student's "failure."

16 Tasks to Be Accomplished as the School Year Progresses

(APRIL)

Review the list of tasks that are typically performed each week and each month:

> (Standard 3) (E) (M) (H)
> These lists appear in Modules 7 and 8, respectively.

Conduct and document formal observations of and conferences with staff members (as required to satisfy time stipulations within the master contract):

> (Standard 2) (Standard 3) (E) (M) (H)
> Maintain a record-keeping system to meet your supervisory and evaluative responsibilities with *both* certified and noncertified employees.

Conduct inservice training sessions with those staff members who will proctor the (May) Proficiency tests:

> (Standard 3) (Standard 2) (E) (M) (H)

Prepare for any end-of-year award and recognition programs for students:

> (Standard 2) (Standard 4) (Standard 3) (E) (M) (H)

MODULE 16: **85**
TASKS TO BE
ACCOMPLISHED
AS THE
SCHOOL YEAR
PROGRESSES
(APRIL)

- Review award categories.
- Review qualification standards.
- Announce and remind staff of pertinent details including the categories and standards.
- Identify recipients. (Provide means for teachers and sponsors to submit names.)
- Confirm sufficient inventory of awards to be presented (if they are to be supplied by the administration).
- Identify person(s) who will present the awards and recognition.
- Based on the number of awards to be presented, calculate the length (time) of the awards assembly, and develop and announce the schedule, including any changes to be made to the regular class schedule.

Prepare for staff evaluation of principal:

(Standard 1) (Standard 5) (E) (M) (H)

In some districts, the master contract or administrative policy requires a formal evaluation of the principal by the staff. If this is the case in your situation, consult with existing guidelines and initiate the appropriate steps. If a staff evaluation of your performance is not required, seek the counsel of an experienced administrator before initiating such action on your own.

Identify probable staff vacancies for the next school year:

(Standard 3) (E) (M) (H)

Initiate steps to fill vacancies, including the following:

- Inform any other administrators involved in the recruitment and selection of personnel.
- Determine the procedure for (1) the posting of such vacancies, (2) the identification and recruitment of qualified candidates, and (3) the selection of new personnel.

Continue to monitor the "End-of-School-Year Checklist for the Principal" (introduced in the "March" tasks in Module 15) and take appropriate action steps:

(Standard 3) (E) (M) (H)

Plan any "end-of-the-year" spirit activities:

(Standard 2) (Standard 3) (E) (M) (H)

If not previously determined, ascertain the district's time frame for submitting appropriation and budgetary requests for the next school year:

(Standard 3) (Standard 2) (Standard 1) (E) (M) (H)

If the district's time frame for submitting appropriation and budgetary requests for the next school year applies to this month, involve staff in identifying needs:

(Standard 3) (Standard 2) (Standard 1) (E) (M) (H)

This includes paper orders, plan books, grade books, glue, textbooks, and so forth.

Identify procedures related to submitting budgetary requests for the next school year:

(Standard 3) (Standard 2) (Standard 1) (E) (M) (H)

To determine budgetary needs, consider factors such as the following:

- Age, condition of existing materials
- Anticipated student enrollment
- Curricular developments (Are any new programs and materials being implemented?)

In addition, you will need to perform the following tasks:

- Project the probable amount of available funds—district budget, principal's account, donated funds (home-school group?).
- Determine the deadline for all purchase orders to be delivered to the central office.
- Establish and inform staff of the procedure for determining the allocation of funds (i.e., who decides how much money is given to whom? Will staff members be involved? Are there criteria for allocating funds?).
- Estimate and inform staff of the time frame for submitting requests for funds.
- Determine availability of and provide all necessary forms.
- Distribute any forms related to staff requests for donated funds.

Tasks to Be Accomplished as the School Year Progresses 17

(MAY)

Review the list of tasks that are typically performed each week and each month:

(Standard 3) (E) (M) (H)
These lists appear in Modules 7 and 8, respectively.

Administer the state Proficiency tests:

(Standard 2) (Standard 3) (E) (M) (H)

Conduct and document formal observations of and conferences with staff members (as required to satisfy time stipulations within the master contract):

(Standard 2) (Standard 3) (E) (M) (H)
Maintain a record-keeping system to meet your supervisory and evaluative responsibilities with *both* certified and noncertified employees.

Identify probable staff vacancies for the next school year:

(Standard 3) (E) (M) (H)
Initiate the following steps to fill such vacancies:

- Inform any other administrators involved in the recruitment and selection of personnel.
- Monitor and verify (1) the posting of such vacancies, (2) the identification and recruitment of qualified candidates, and (3) the selection and employment of new personnel.

As provided by district procedure, participate in the process of interviewing candidates for staff vacancies:

(Standard 3) (Standard 1) (Standard 2) (E) (M) (H)

Inform students and parents of any overdue fee payments and the related policy:

(Standard 3) (E) (M) (H)

Monitor plans for any "end-of-the-school-year" spirit activities:

(Standard 2) (Standard 3) (E) (M) (H)

Continue work related to the budget for the next school year:

(Standard 3) (Standard 2) (Standard 1) (E) (M) (H)

- Review the task statement for budget responsibility as listed in Module 16 and verify that all tasks have been completed.
- Collect all, or as many as possible, requests for budgetary funds.
- Decide, with appropriate involvement of other staff members, the allocation of funds.
- Monitor the preparation of approved purchase orders.
- Sign and deliver all approved purchase orders to the appropriate individual or department.

Continue to monitor the "End-of-School-Year Checklist for the Principal" (introduced in the "March" tasks in Module 15) and take appropriate action steps:

(Standard 3) (E) (M) (H)

Conduct orientation program(s) for incoming students and their parents:

(Standard 1) (Standard 2) (Standard 3) (Standard 4) (E) (M) (H)

MODULE 17: **89**
TASKS TO BE
ACCOMPLISHED
AS THE
SCHOOL
YEAR PROGRESSES
(MAY)

Prepare the calendar for the next school year:

(Standard 3) (E) (M) (H)

Review the calendar for the current school year and any notes you have filed in your "Next Year" folder. Invite other school stakeholders to contribute to the new calendar.

Review and implement appropriate action steps related to the "End-of-School-Year Checklist for Teachers"

(Standard 3) (E) (M) (H)

The following table (see Table 12) shows a sample memo you can use to inform teachers of duties they need to complete before leaving for summer vacation. Before distributing the memo, fill in the appropriate information where you see the underlined, italicized phrases within parentheses that call for insertions.

Table 12

End-of-School-Year Checklist for Teachers

MEMO

(Insert date)

TO: All teachers

FROM: *(Insert your name)*

RE: End-of-School-Year Checklist for Teachers

Before leaving on *(insert date):*

___ 1. Return your copy of the building or district handbook to *(insert location or person).*

___ 2. Compile a list of repairs that need attention in your room or area and submit the list to *(insert location and/or person).*

___ 3. Store all student textbooks and teacher's editions *(insert location and procedure).*

___ 4. Secure all computers and audio-visual equipment *(insert location and procedure).*

___ 5. Clear all surfaces (desks, walls, cabinets, etc.) within your teaching area and faculty planning area so that the custodians or cleaning staff may clean.

___ 6. Submit all school keys to *(specify the location or person).*

___ 7. If you have textbooks to be rebound and have received approval for budget appropriations, label and deliver such textbooks *(specify the procedure)* to *(specify the location or person).*

___ 8. Complete and submit the "Summer Contact" sheet and the self-addressed envelope to *(specify the location or person).*

___ 9. After checking off the completed items on this "End-of-School-Year Checklist for Teachers," sign and date it below and submit it to *(specify the location or person).*

TEACHER SIGNATURE: _____

DATE: _____

Tasks to Be Accomplished as the School Year Progresses 18

(JUNE)

Review the list of tasks that are typically performed each week and each month:

(Standard 3) (E) (M) (H)
These lists appear in Modules 7 and 8, respectively.

Finalize work related to the budget for the next school year:

(Standard 3) (Standard 2) (Standard 1) (E) (M) (H)

- Review the task statements for budget responsibility as listed in Module 15 to verify that all such tasks have been completed.
- Collect any remaining requests for budgetary funds.
- Monitor the preparation of approved purchase orders.
- Sign and deliver all approved purchase orders to the appropriate individual or department.

Conduct any "end-of-the-school-year" spirit activities:

(Standard 2) (Standard 3) (E) (M) (H)

Conduct end-of-year award and recognition programs for students:

(Standard 2) (Standard 4) (Standard 3) (E) (M) (H)

Identify probable staff vacancies for the next school year:

(Standard 3) (E) (M) (H)
Initiate the following steps to fill such vacancies:

- Inform any other administrators involved in the recruitment and selection of personnel.
- Monitor and verify (1) the posting of such vacancies, (2) the identification and recruitment of qualified candidates, and (3) the selection and employment of new personnel.

As provided by district procedure, participate in the process of interviewing candidates for staff vacancies:

(Standard 3) (Standard 1) (Standard 2) (E) (M) (H)

Review, initiate, and monitor the process for printing and mailing the fourth-quarter, end-of-year pupil progress reports:

(Standard 2) (Standard 3) (E) (M) (H)

- You may delegate various aspects of this task; however, grade reporting is so important and sensitive that you need to monitor the accuracy and efficiency of the process very carefully.
- If policy so provides, place a "hold" on the progress reports of students who owe school fees. Inform the parents or guardians of the pupils whose reports are being held that the reports will not be sent until they make restitution, and explain the procedure for late payment and release of the reports. If your district provides waivers of fees for destitute families, provide that information in a tactful manner.

Complete and submit any required "end-of-year" reports:

(Standard 3) (E) (M) (H)

- Determine if local or state entities require you to submit "end-of-year" reports.
- If such reports are required, determine if you need information from other staff members before they depart for the summer.
- Verify the collection of all information from staff and the completion of all tasks by staff as specified in the "end-of-year" checklists previously distributed.

Tasks to Be Accomplished for the Next School Year 19

(JULY–AUGUST)

Complete follow-up activities to any tasks of preceding months, and prepare for those tasks listed for the ensuing months:

(Standard 3) (E) (M) (H)

Review existing policies and procedures:

(Standard 3) (E) (M) (H)

Consult with the central office personnel if you wish to recommend any changes to the Board of Education policy manual and the school district's administrative procedures handbook.

Analyze the academic performance record of the school, and map your leadership strategies accordingly:

(Standard 2) (E) (M) (H)

Depending on the school's performance record, you will need to consult with the appropriate personnel to develop strategies that further the academic performance of the students.

Review handbooks for staff and students:

(Standard 3) (E) (M) (H)

- Verify that the content in the building handbooks is consistent with the policies and procedures outlined in the Board of Education policy manual, the school district's administrative procedures handbook, and the Master Contracts or Agreements that exist between various labor groups and the Board of Education.
- Review and prepare building-level handbooks for printing.
- Authorize the printing of such building-level handbooks and prepare copies for distribution.

Monitor the repair and maintenance of the physical facility:

(Standard 3) (E) (M) (H)

Monitor the status of staffing needs:

(Standard 3) (E) (M) (H)

Be prepared to participate in job interviews as vacancies occur and the personnel office identifies candidates.

Review active purchase orders and verify the presence, or scheduled delivery, of all necessary physical materials:

(Standard 3) (E) (M) (H)

- For faculty and staff: teaching manuals, instructional materials, equipment, supplies, furniture, and so on.
- For students: textbooks, desks and chairs, and so on.

Analyze the readiness of the building:

(Standard 3) (Standard 4) (E) (M) (H)

- Monitor work scheduled for completion during the summer. Determine if there are any work orders not completed. Make certain that repairs requested by staff are completed or that a plan for completion exists.
- Meet regularly with the custodian(s) to monitor the cleaning and repair of the facility.

Develop the master schedule:

(Standard 3) (E) (M) (H)

Analyze the needs for the upcoming school year. Review the schedules of each teacher. Confirm the complete and accurate scheduling of *each* student. After you confirm the number of students and teachers for the new school year, verify that class enrollments are as balanced as possible;

MODULE 19: **95**
TASKS TO BE
ACCOMPLISHED
FOR THE NEXT
SCHOOL YEAR
(JULY–AUGUST)

classroom assignments (for students and teachers) are accurate; and adequate furniture is in place.

RECOMMENDED READINGS RELATED TO "DOING THE JOB"

Call them strategies, techniques, tools, tips, or tricks of the trade, this second part of *The Portable Mentor* has demonstrated that there are certain specific things you need to know as you go about "doing the job" as school principal. In addition to the tasks identified in Part II of this book, the publications listed below elaborate on how to perform those job-specific tasks that principals—especially entry-year principals—must accomplish. To expand your repertoire, I recommend including the following texts in your collection of professional reading material.

I am reluctant to list these books by any priority, as all of them make valuable contributions to the profession. However, I will cite one in particular: the Glickman book on "Supervision of Instruction," which is a great text for aspiring administrators. When using this book with college courses, I encourage students to keep it as a reference tool they can use on the job. As a measure of its widespread acceptance, notice that this book is a fourth-edition printing. It is an excellent compilation of knowledge related to supervision of instruction, which is a *major* responsibility for school principals.

The other Glickman book listed (*Leadership for Learning: How to Help Teachers Succeed*) focuses on what you as the principal can do to facilitate the performance of teachers. Two quotations from this publication summarize the significance of a principal's role in leading for learning. "Research has found that faculty in successful schools always question existing instructional practice and do not blame lack of student achievement on external causes" (page 4), and "The 'source of the problem' in ordinary schools is always someone else: the students, the parents and caretakers, the school board, and so on" (page 6). In two sentences, Glickman squarely links the responsibility for student learning with school leadership.

Charlotte Danielson's book on enhancing student achievement provides an orderly, sequential process for school principals to provide such leadership. Her four-point model ("What we want, what we believe, what we know, and what we do") cogently guides efforts toward comprehensive school improvement. The section on "what we know" provides a succinct summary of relevant research.

All learning, of course, relates to the human brain, and all instructional leaders need to be aware of brain research. Sousa's book is a great starting point. Schmoker's two books offer direction for improving school performance; his "Results Fieldbook" details strategies used by schools that realized dramatic improvement. Carr and Harris explain a process that schools can use to improve student performance by linking curriculum, assessment, and "action planning." Marzano focuses on translating

research into action by identifying factors that influence student learning
and then offering ideas for dealing with those forces.

Before you go too far down the road of improving test scores, I urge
you to read Popham's book regarding "the truth about testing." While illu-
minating the errors and absurdities surrounding many of the conclusions
drawn from tests and test scores, he provides options for improving the
measurement malaise.

Daresh's book on beginning the principalship complements this publication with checklists and planning sheets for personal and professional
growth. Additional insights, anecdotes, and advice about the principalship
are available in the Schumaker and Sommers text. Eppler's book about
how to avoid "management mess-ups," while not limited to school administration, offers some solid managerial advice.

Challenges abound for school leaders and among them are "difficult"
teachers, a topic taken on in Whitaker's book. Seeking consensus among
people with different agendas is another challenge for the group leader;
the book by Ness and Hoffman describes numerous inservice activities
and provides worksheets to help a group establish the environment and
skills necessary to achieve consensus. Conners makes a strong point
regarding the importance of affirming the contributions of staff members
and points out that leaders often fail because they underestimate the
power of praise. Owen's book on "Open Space Technology" describes a
unique approach that leaders can use with groups to "combine the level of
synergy and excitement present in a good coffee break with the substan-
tive activity and results characteristic of a good meeting" (page 3).

Central—and common—to "doing the job" is the element of *time*; you
are certain to hear others—and probably yourself—say, "When do I do all
of these things?" The text by Adelman, Walking Eagle, and Hargreaves
serves as a springboard for discussion about appropriate use of time in
relation to school reform. Of course, no discussion of time management
would be complete without acknowledging the "oldie but goodie" publication of *The One-Minute Manager*; Blanchard and Johnson's treatise on
time management still holds good advice for all persons interested in
making the most of the time that is available.

* * *

Adelman, N. E., Walking Eagle, K. P., & Hargreaves, A. (1997). *Racing With the
Clock: Making Time for Teaching and Learning in School Reform*. New York:
Teachers College Press.
Blanchard, K., & Johnson, S. (1981). *The One Minute Manager*. New York: Penquin
Putnam.
Carr, J. F., & Harris, D. E. (2001). *Succeeding With Standards: Linking Curriculum,
Assessment, and Action Planning*. Alexandria, VA: The Association for
Supervision and Curriculum Development.
Conners, N. A. (2000). *If You Don't Feed the Teachers They Eat the Students: A Guide
to Success for Administrators and Teachers*. Nashville, TN: Incentive.
Danielson, C. (2002). *Enhancing Student Achievement: A Framework for School
Improvement*. Alexandria, VA: The Association for Supervision and
Curriculum Improvement.

MODULE 19: 97
TASKS TO BE
ACCOMPLISHED
FOR THE NEXT
SCHOOL YEAR
(JULY–AUGUST)

Daresh, J. C. (2001). *Beginning the Principalship: A Practical Guide for New School Leaders* (2nd ed.). Thousand Oaks, CA: Corwin.

Eppler, M. (1997). *Management Mess-Ups: 57 Pitfalls You Can Avoid (and Stories of Those Who Don't)*. Franklin Lakes, NJ: Career Press.

Glickman, C. D. (2002). *Leadership for Learning: How to Help Teachers Succeed.* Alexandria, VA: The Association for Supervision and Curriculum Development.

Glickman, C. D., Gordon, S., & Ross-Gordon, J. (1998). *Supervision of Instruction: A Developmental Approach* (4th ed.). Boston: Allyn & Bacon.

Marzano, R. (2003). *What Works in Schools—Translating Research Into Action.* Alexandria, VA: The Association for Supervision and Curriculum Development.

Ness, J., & Hoffman, C. (1998). *Putting Sense Into Consensus.* Tacoma, WA: Vista.

Owen, H. (1977). *Open Space Technology—A User's Guide* (2nd ed.). San Francisco: Berrett-Koehler.

Popham, W. J. (2001). *The Truth About Testing: An Educator's Call to Action.* Alexandria, VA: The Association for Supervision and Curriculum Development.

Schmoker, M. J. (1999). *Results: The Key to Continuous School Improvement.* Alexandria, VA: The Association for Supervision and Curriculum Development.

Schmoker, M. J. (2001). *The Results Fieldbook: Practical Strategies From Dramatically Improved Schools.* Alexandria, VA: The Association for Supervision and Curriculum Development.

Schumaker, D. R., & Sommers, W. A. (2001). *Being a Successful Principal: Riding the Wave of Change Without Drowning.* Thousands Oaks, CA: Corwin.

Sousa, D. R. (1995). *How the Brain Learns.* Reston, VA: The National Association of Secondary School Principals.

Whitaker, T. (1999). *Dealing With Difficult Teachers.* Larchmont, NY: Eye on Education.

Part III

Deciphering the Job

Fred's Handy-Dandy "A to Z" List of Tips for the Entry-Year Principal

20

If you have followed the path that I laid out in the previous parts of this handbook, then you have walked through a definition of the principal's role in Part I and examined the tasks related to doing the job in Part II. So, now comes this third part, which I call "deciphering the job." According to Webster, to decipher is to "translate into ordinary, understandable language" or "to make out the meaning of," which is what I offer in this section. The following experientially based conclusions or "lessons learned" have broad application to the challenges associated with being the school leader. You can use this section for personal reflection as well as a conversation starter with your mentor (if you have one) and other school administrators.

Aardvark

Relax; there is no direct correlation between an aardvark and being a principal. This is just a way to start an "A to Z" list with a word that begins with the letter "A"—and it tests your sense of humor, which you will definitely need if you are going to survive as a school principal.

Abbreviations and Acronyms

When communicating with the public, explain—or better yet, avoid—pedagogical abbreviations and acronyms. Educators commonly speak of

ACT, ADA, ADHD, ETS, IAT, IDEA, IEP, IGE, IMC, LD, PTA, PTC, PTO, SAT, and . . . well, you probably get the idea.

Advice Giving

•   Do not "push the river." Emergencies and liabilities aside, resist the temptation to offer unsolicited advice. Rushing in to solve the perceived problems of another will rob the other person of the opportunity to resolve his or her problems or issues. This can retard the other person's ability to develop self-reliance.

•   Advice giving may also have repercussions for you; that is, if things go poorly, the person to whom you gave advice may respond by saying, "Remember, *you* told me I should . . ."

Advice Seeking (Two Rules!)

- Rule Number 1: When faced with dilemmas and decision making, if you have the time, seek the advice of others.
- Rule Number 2: When faced with dilemmas and decision making, *make the time* to seek the advice of others.

True, you really cannot "make" time. However, you are responsible for how you *use* your time. By allotting time to seek advice, you can acquire perspectives and information that you may currently lack. You may also enhance your relationship with those from whom you seek advice, as people often feel complimented when asked for their opinion. You do not diminish your leadership stature, nor do you relinquish your authority, by asking for advice, because after gathering such input, you still are the one who must ultimately make the final decision.

Anticipation

- Anticipate as much as you can without making yourself paranoid.
- Mentally "walk through" an event before it occurs; consider "what if?" scenarios and develop contingency plans.

Assumptions

- Making assumptions can be troublesome, for you and for others.
- Assume as little as possible and remember the corny joke about what happens when you "assume."

Authority

Short of being willing to submit your resignation as proof of your personal convictions, your authority is dependent upon the support of the superintendent and the Board of Education. Be aware of and sensitive to their respective positions on issues before you speak or take action.

MODULE 20: **103**
FRED'S HANDY-
DANDY "A TO Z"
LIST OF TIPS FOR
THE ENTRY-YEAR
PRINCIPAL

Change

• There is an expression that says there is no "I" in the word "team." Similarly, there is no "y" in the word "change," but perhaps there should be. Why should there be a "y" in "change"? Because, whenever you suggest or plan changing something, the first question you should be prepared to answer is, "Why?" Because people will want to know "why," it is important that you first establish the *need* to change, not just in your own mind, but also in the minds of others involved in the change.

• Faced with the realities of rank (i.e., authority, coercion, and other similar "offers that can't be refused"), even the most reluctant of staff members can be compelled to adopt some form of change for some period of time. However, if you want to bring about effective and long-lasting change in something that involves other people, those other people are more likely to help you accomplish the change and support it over time if they *recognize and accept the need* to change and *support the methods* of changing. In a word, for others to adopt change in a meaningful manner, they must possess a "readiness" to change.

Collegiality

As often as possible, be supportive of others, especially fellow administrators. We administrators have enough critics without our publicly second-guessing each other.

Commitment or Promises

• *Before* you commit to or promise something, be certain that you can do it.
• *After* you commit to or promise something, be certain that you do what you committed to or promised. This is especially true when you are dealing with disciplinary matters involving students.

Communication Skills

There really is an entire body of knowledge in this area. The more you know and master about communication, the greater the success that you will experience as you interact with other people. I have assembled some information on this topic in the following module titled, "Communication Skills That Many People Talk About, But . . ."

Confrontation

• Do not be reluctant to deal with issues promptly (see "Procrastination").
• Confronting the other person privately is usually the wisest choice.
• There can be some benefit to public confrontation; however, there are costs associated with it. Rationally weigh the consequences before you act.

"Da Boss"

- Determine what your supervisor or evaluator ("da boss") wants of you.
- Ascertain if there are any "pet projects," special needs, or interests that your boss values. Learn how he or she wants you to operate. Learn her or his priorities and values and be thankful if the two of you agree on these points. Granted, it is best if you can determine this before taking the job, but unfortunately, you usually have to be in the position for a time to learn these things. At the very least, be aware of the need to learn this information and pay attention to it as you serve on the job.
- Determine if your supervisor wants to be directly involved in decisions related to particular situations or circumstances.

Decision Making

- Decide how you are going to decide.
- If you are going to involve others in decision making, have a formal, fair, and consistent way to do so. Be sure others know and understand your system of decision making.
- Be cautious about making decisions that will set a precedent. You will probably have to do this on occasion; just be certain that you have thought through the possible implications of your decision.
- Whenever possible, buy yourself some time. Not every problem needs an immediate answer or solution.
- A decision-making riddle:

  Question: Five frogs are sitting on a log. Four of the frogs decide to jump off. How many frogs are left sitting on the log?

  Answer: Five. Why? Because there is a difference between "deciding" and "doing."

Disciplining of Students

- When deciding your response to a student's misconduct, think "logical consequences," that is, link the consequences to the student's misconduct. This may require some creativity on your part, but keep in mind that your goal is to modify the student's behavior. When the same students repeat the same or similar acts of misconduct and we routinely respond with the same consequences, might we not conclude that the consequences are ineffective?

- There are different types of misconduct. Here is one way to classify student misconduct: Consider whether the student's behavior is (a) detrimental to others (i.e., disruptive to the instructional and learning process or dangerous to the welfare of others) or (b) detrimental only to herself or himself.

MODULE 20: **105**
FRED'S HANDY-
DANDY "A TO Z"
LIST OF TIPS FOR
THE ENTRY-YEAR
PRINCIPAL

- Recognizing and valuing the distinction between these types of misconduct should lead to different types of responses.

- Whenever possible, enact discipline that produces an improvement in the student's behavior.

Documentation

- Value paper trails—establish and maintain records of your work and communiqués.
- As you start a new position, look for records that may provide some perspective on the job, culture, history, and expectations.

Failure

- Short of total disaster, we can learn valuable lessons from "failure."
- Young people especially need opportunities to learn that they can overcome what they perceive as "failure." They often lack the perspective that they can bounce back, recover, and persevere. As you interact with students (and their parents) during situations that the students perceive as overwhelming, you may be able to promote this perspective by offering examples of persons who overcame seemingly insurmountable obstacles. Your support may help a young person stay the course and learn that good can come from things that we initially perceive as bad.

Favorites

Avoid *all* appearances that you have any favorites among the staff, students, or parents.

Group-Process Skills

If your formal education did not include this subject and you desire to learn about it, you may have to search for it yourself—but the payoff can be worth it. I have included some information to whet your appetite in the module titled, "Things Momma Never Told Me About Working With People."

Gut

Sometimes you just have to trust your own.

Humility

- Schools are human organizations. It takes the combined efforts of many people to create and maintain a successful operation. One person (such as the principal) does not an organization make.

- To retain your sense of humility, remember the void that you create when you remove your fist from bucket of water. More than likely, school was in session before you arrived and school will be in session after you leave.

Humor, Sense of

You had best have one. Be willing to laugh at yourself and your errors (that way, you are more likely to be laughing when others are).

Judgment

Reserve judgment; do not simply accept the views and interpretations of others as the way things are or should be. Some of the most loyal, well-meaning individuals will present situations to you in terms influenced by their own biases or perspectives.

Leadership Style

- Be aware that more than one style exists.
- Determine which one you are using and question whether it is the right one for you and the circumstances.

Leadership Versus Management

While many distinguished individuals have written volumes that distinguish between leadership and management, I do not believe that this is an "either-or" proposition. To succeed as the school leader, you must manage *and* lead or lead *and* manage.

Management System

- Be aware that more than one exists.
- Determine which one you are using and question whether it is the right one for you and the circumstances.

Mistakes

- Mistakes are similar to hiccups; occasionally, everyone experiences them.
- Almost all mistakes are correctable.
- The reality that everyone makes mistakes and that most errors are correctable is an *extremely* important message for young people, who typically lack this perspective.
- As a school leader, you should expect mistakes, which is not the same as accepting them. Plan well and try to avoid errors. When errors occur, take steps to avoid making the same mistake again.

MODULE 20: **107**
FRED'S HANDY-
DANDY "A TO Z"
LIST OF TIPS FOR
THE ENTRY-YEAR
PRINCIPAL

"My School" Versus "Our School"

- Reflect on the possible leadership and management perspective of the principal who consistently uses the phrase "my school."
- Reflect on the possible leadership and management perspective of the principal who consistently uses the phrase "our school."
- Consciously decide which phrase you want to use.

"New Kid on the Block" Assessment

If you want to conduct a quick and informal assessment of the values and attitudes that group members (i.e., staff members) hold about past, present, and future practices at the school, you may want to consider using the following "Stop, Keep, Start" strategy. You can use this survey technique for other topics and groups besides the faculty (e.g., student groups, parent groups, and other employee groups).

Ask all members of the group to privately record their responses to the following questions:

1. What things are done at the school that you want to **Stop** doing?

2. What things are done at the school that you want to **Keep** doing?

3. What things are not done at the school that you want to **Start** doing?

The number of group members you will need to survey may influence your method. For example, if it's a small group, you could meet with each member and discuss that person's responses to the questions. Another approach would be to collect the written responses and initiate the tabulation and analysis of the data.

"Off the Record" Comments

When you are the principal, you can never speak "off the record." Others are apt to interpret and relay (i.e., quote) anything you say as, "But the principal said . . ."

Partiality

Be fair with others, especially when dealing with money, judgments, and favors (see "Favorites" above).

Plan

- Use a planning calendar. (The operative word here is "use." Do not just have one to carry around or look good on your desk.)
- Mentally "walk through" the steps involved in an activity. Are all of them covered?

- Prepare; pay attention to details.
- Maintain a "next year" or "next time" file. Drop notes into it about things you may want to change, research, and so forth.

Popularity

Do not chase it. If you are to have it, it will come to you.

Prioritize

- Develop the ability to prioritize.
- Develop the habit of prioritizing.

(Be) Proactive

- Meet issues head-on; take the initiative. For example, if some unfortunate or unpleasant incident occurs that involves school stakeholders, then to the best of your ability and control, be sure that you are the first to deliver the news. For example—and this is especially true when dealing with those parents who say, "My child doesn't lie to me"—make the telephone call to that parent *before* he or she hears the story from someone else, that is, the child.

- Encourage other staff members to be similarly proactive.

Problem Ownership

- *Learn* the concept of problem ownership!
- *Remember* the concept of problem ownership!
- *Use* the concept of problem ownership!

If I could magically snap my fingers to grant you one power, one skill, or one ability for you to use in your role of school leader, it would be the mastery of this concept: problem ownership. In your role as school principal, you can use the concept of problem ownership dozens of time every day! Problem ownership is a powerful tool for anyone who runs the "complaint department" of the school, that is, the principal's office. For more thoughts regarding problem ownership, see the "Things Momma Never Told Me About Working With People" module that follows.

Procrastination

- Avoid it . . . by attacking it.
- Usually, the anxiety about doing some unpleasant task is worse than the task itself. The longer you put if off, the more difficult it becomes, so avoid, or reduce, such anxiety by doing the difficult as soon as possible.

MODULE 20: **109**
FRED'S HANDY-
DANDY "A TO Z"
LIST OF TIPS FOR
THE ENTRY-YEAR
PRINCIPAL

Professionalism

It seems safe to say that we all want others to like us. Professional literature promotes the concept of the principal operating in a "welcoming" manner. Nonetheless, while projecting an approachable, "open" manner, I believe that it is important to maintain a professional distance with others whom you supervise. It is especially important to avoid acts that might suggest favoritism toward others.

Proofreading

You are responsible for the accuracy and correctness of any printed material that carries your name. Proofread it yourself, always, but if it is particularly important, have a second pair of eyes look at it, too.

Purpose

Frequently ask yourself and others with whom you work, "What is the purpose of this activity? Why are we, or why am I, doing this?" Asking (and answering) this question provides focus. The answer(s) can clarify and give direction. This question ("What is the purpose of this activity?") applies to both administrative and instructional issues.

Readiness

Develop the ability to read the readiness of a situation and the readiness of others in the situation. This ability to sense readiness applies to several aspects of leadership (see "Change" and "Staff Development Programs").

Record Keeping

- Date all documents sent and received.
- Do not be in a rush to discard documents.

Reprimands

- Reprimands are best served in private.
- Avoid the "shotgun" approach (speaking or writing to everyone when the problem or issue involves only one individual or a few persons).
- Gather accurate information before acting.
- Allow explanations; seek explanations. Give the other person a chance to explain his or her perspective or reasoning. You may want to open with a remark such as, "Help me understand why . . ."
- Talk first; write second. Do not automatically commit initial reprimands to written form. Try talking with the other person(s) and, if possible, avoid initiating a "paper war."

Respect

Perform so that others will respect you. Do not pursue popularity; the only place where popularity comes before respect is in the dictionary.

Sacred Cows

- Accurately and quickly assess the culture (values, attitudes, habits, traditions, etc.) of the building and community.
- Determine if there are any "sacred cows." If there are, proceed very cautiously, especially if your plans will result in the wounding or death of any of them.

Staff Development Programs

- Do not assume that you know what the staff needs or what is best for the staff to learn. Involve the staff in developing inservice programs.
- Do not assume that you can hire and schedule an "expert" from outside the school or district to come in with a one-time application and "fix" the problem or address the need that you perceive. Sometimes the best resources are current staff members.
- Do not assume that you can resolve serious needs in short order.
- Do not expect long-lasting results, if you do not involve the staff in diagnosing, designing, and delivering the staff development program.

"Zee" Final Point

When faced with aggravations, frustrations, irritations, vexations, and all other manner of "ations," try to remember: "This too shall pass."

Things Momma Never Told Me About Working With People 21

Okay, you finished the course work, you obtained your license, you survived the interviews, the Board of Education named you principal, and you have a grasp of the tasks that you need to accomplish. Now you lead and the teachers follow, right? Well . . . perhaps not, for there are other dimensions to the job, as suggested in this section.

A *major* part of the principal's role involves working with groups of people

Listening to how some of them talk, one might well assume that the school principal functions like a kingmaker—pulling strings, moving chess pieces, deploying the troops like a field marshal. This type of principal often peppers his or her language with phrases like, "at my school," or "my teachers," or "my students," or "my budget," or "I decided . . ."

In reality, few acts of school leadership are accomplished in isolation. While the school principal is singularly responsible for many aspects of the school's operation, achieving the vast majority of those things depends on the principal's ability to accomplish goals by working with others.

Having your name on the letterhead does not guarantee that others will follow you

While those who interviewed and employed you may be ecstatic about you becoming the new principal, there is a strong probability that some staff members will be less enthusiastic. These are the "wait and see" types who are skeptical about you, your plans, and your mode of operation. Yes, your qualifications for the role of school leader may be impeccable and your preservice training may have been superb. Yes, you may be extremely knowledgeable about current hot topics and vital issues in education. Yes, your principal preparation program may have provided great insight and valuable information about pertinent school-related topics: curriculum, instruction, leadership, school improvement, school law, personnel, and so forth. Yes, you may be well qualified with cognitive data. However, once on the job, theory meets practice and dreams encounter reality.

As you set about to lead staff, students, parents, and other community members in the crusade to improve the school's performance, you probably will face the challenge of working with some individuals and groups who may not share the same vision as you. That is when the realization sets in: *They are not automatically following my lead! Now what do I do?* When you start searching for ways to accomplish organizational goals through working with others, especially adults, I suggest that you consider the following points.

Working with groups of people, while challenging, can be very rewarding

You may know exactly what the school needs. You may already have, before collecting any input or feedback from anyone else, an accurate and feasible plan to move the school in the proper direction. However, the ethos of modern-day school administration demands that you lead in a collaborative manner. Thus, in your quest to bring about meaningful change, you must cooperatively set agendas, mutually establish vision and mission statements, gather opinions, seek consensus, persuade, convince, and even cajole others to join you in your efforts to bring about change.

Achieving progress through others can be difficult work. Experienced principals report the obvious—the hours are long and the duties demanding; criticism is plentiful and appreciation scarce. So, why does anyone want to become a school leader?

Some persons may aspire to be the leader because they observed someone who displayed great leadership skills and they desire to follow that person's example. Alternatively, it may be a matter of "I want to make a difference in the lives of students." Or, perhaps it struck you one day that somebody has to be the leader and you believe that you can do as well as, or better than, someone that you observed in the leadership role. Regardless of your reason for becoming the school principal, if you do make a positive contribution to the lives of students, parents, and staff members, then that realization is a powerful and rewarding sensation. *Have no doubt about it—being a school principal can be a very fulfilling experience.*

Working with groups of people, while rewarding, can be very challenging

Individuals and groups have their own agendas and sometimes those agendas conflict with the goals and direction of the leaders and the organization. When those agendas differ, conflict occurs and life becomes less pleasant, particularly for the person who tries to keep everyone on the same page, focused on the same goals, and unified in purpose. *Have no doubt about it; being a school principal can be a very challenging experience.*

Being a cheerleader may not be enough

Some who aspire to become school principals stress how they plan to "rally the troops"; build a spirit of camaraderie; and shower individuals and groups with rewards, compliments, and other forms of positive feedback that will increase motivation and achieve a sense of unity, purpose, and accomplishment! While these are laudable aspirations, not all staff members will be won over by such euphoric efforts. The willingness to confront such individuals and effectively communicate with them about their concerns and issues is a desirable trait and necessary skill for school principals.

Making decisions is central to the job

Ultimately, as the principal, you get to (or have to) decide many issues. The magic in the process is what you do *before* you decide. How do you arrive at decisions? Do you flip coins, draw straws, or throw darts at the "yes-no" chart on the wall? Do you decide alone? Do you allow others to provide input? If so, whom do you include? Moreover, how do you make the decision if the input from others is mixed or inconclusive? Do you know and are you capable of displaying the leadership skills necessary to achieve consensus among persons who hold differing views on an issue; or, do you forego attempts at consensus building and revert to voting? If so, do the group members vote in secret or in the open? Who counts the votes? These are but a few of the procedural and operational factors that should be determined before you attempt to resolve specific issues.

Running a faculty meeting is risky business

Some principals attempt to arrive at decisions by employing the spirit of the "town meeting," that is, holding a faculty meeting to determine what to do. Be advised that if your goal is to reach consensus in a meeting of the entire faculty, you may be seeking the impossible. Allowing open discussion and trying to arrive at a decision in such a setting may not be the wisest approach to group decision making. Often, a few of the more vocal individuals will dominate and thus limit the full range of discussion. There are other ways to organize staff input and assure that all staff member have the opportunity to participate in the decisions that affect them. See the Guidelines for Participatory Management, which appear in Part II, Module 5, under the heading, *Develop a planned, organized approach to decision making.*

Middle management is a
lonely way to make a living

As you assume the role of the school principal, be prepared to experience a sense of isolation, especially if you are the only administrator in the building. Be wary of speaking confidentially with staff members about issues involving other staff members. It is essential that the principal demonstrate professional discretion in all job-related contacts.

In addition, being a school principal requires that you have several allegiances; after all, the principalship is middle management. You must be supportive of at least two, and sometimes more, separate and occasionally discordant forces at the same time: the building staff and the central office staff, which includes your boss, the superintendent. This dilemma is another reason for you to nurture collegial relationships with other school principals who know and appreciate the loneliness of the position and may be able to offer helpful advice.

Developing a "thick skin" is helpful

Expect criticism—it comes with the territory. No one can expect to satisfy all the people all the time. Over time, you will acquire your share of critics. Again, having a sense of problem ownership will help you cope. Above all else, use your sense of what is right for the students as a compass for determining the proper direction and making the right decisions.

Be optimistic, but accept
disappointment as part of the job

Schools are human organizations; humans occasionally err. From time to time, the actions of others will disappoint you. Expect it, accept it, and move on. This is not to say that you cannot or should not take corrective steps to eliminate whatever caused the disappointment; just do not be surprised when it happens.

The concept of
"problem ownership" is powerful

It is tempting, especially in the early stages of one's career as a building principal, to perceive *all* school-related problems and issues as personal challenges; to accept them as battles to be taken on, defeated, and chalked up as a testament to one's ability to lead, to manage, and to solve problems for others.

Yes, one could argue that all issues, incidents, and situations that occur in the school operation must eventually fall under the province and responsibility of the school principal. However, such a mind-set comes with a price—it can lead to undue stress and possible "burnout" of the principal, and it can foster a climate in which the principal becomes the paternal or maternal decision-making figurehead thus limiting the opportunity for others in the organization to develop their own problem-solving skills.

Even though you must be accountable for the total operation of the school, you do not have to "buy" every problem that is being "sold" to you. People who deliver problems to you sometimes just need you to listen or affirm what they already know they need to do.

When someone presents you with a problematic situation, you can decide whether to accept the problem presented to you by asking yourself how the problem affects you. If the problem interferes with your comfort zone, if it is presented in a way that tangibly or concretely affects how you feel or operate, you may choose to get involved with solving the problem. If, on the other hand, the problem does not have a direct, tangible, concrete impact on you, then you may choose not to accept the problem and may instead choose to take on the role of an "active listener" rather than a "problem solver."

The realization that one may choose whether or not to accept the problem presented is one of the most powerful and liberating experiences that a school principal can have! Appreciating, developing, and maintaining the concept of problem ownership can give you a sense of control, a realization that you have some choice regarding matters that you encounter on the job.

22 Communication Skills That People Talk About, But . . .

The following statement summarizes the dilemma that frequently characterizes communication between individuals or groups:

"I know you believe you understand what you think I said, but I am not sure you realize that what you heard is not what I meant."

(S.I. Hayakawa, semanticist, college president, U.S. senator)

Too often, the failure to listen carefully, to seek clarification of messages received and sent, leads to ineffective communication. Many people talk about "effective communication"; however, as demonstrated by the quotation above, talking about it is not the same as effectively communicating.

Effective communication is central to effective administration

Okay, let us say that you have decided to resist accepting every problem and issue presented to you and you are going to use the concept of problem ownership as you interact with others. How do you not "buy" or assume ownership for every problem presented to you and still demonstrate to others that you care about and value them and their issues? As addressed below, this requires skillful communication.

"And, we're going to improve communications around here!"

It is rather commonplace to hear newly elected or appointed leaders speak of the importance of "good communication." Leaders announce changes to ensure that everyone has a voice in operations, toss out new slogans, disseminate heartfelt memos, and put up flashy posters. Then what happens? Typically, things gradually return to normal, and slowly a new cycle of complaints about poor communication begins to surface.

Why does this happen? Perhaps it is because the leadership perceives communication within an organization as an issue that requires sweeping institutional change. However, results that are more significant and longer lasting will occur when efforts focus on improving communication in the day-to-day, person-to-person context.

The following section provides a cursory review of some effective communication practices that make a difference, especially if the person in charge values, implements, and sustains the habit of using these techniques. These ideas are practical, inexpensive, and effective, if consistently applied.

Be an "active" listener

• When you are an active listener, you *demonstrate* that you are listening by being nonverbally responsive to the person who is speaking. You look at the speaker, maintain eye contact, and nod or tilt your head to indicate that you are being attentive.

• Another part of being an active listener involves understanding what the other person means by his or her comments. You must confirm that you correctly understand by verifying your interpretation of what the other person has said. You can do this by using either of the following approaches:

• Ask clarifying questions:

  – "Is it accurate to say that you believe . . . ?"
  – "Are you saying . . . ?"
  – "Am I correct that you see this situation as . . . ?"
  – "Do you mean that . . . ?"

• Restate the other person's comments to determine if he or she agrees with your interpretation of his or her remarks.

  – "It sounds like you are saying that . . ."
  – "In other words, you believe . . ."
  – "So, from your perspective, the situation appears . . ."
  – "Then, what you are telling me is . . ."

Own your feelings and thoughts

Does this sound familiar?

"You know, they say that when you think about it, you can always tell when they . . ."

This is an example of how some of us fall into the trap of sloppy or lazy speech patterns and unwittingly hide our feelings and thoughts behind the ubiquitous "you" and "they." There are better, more direct ways to communicate that allow us to take responsibility for our thoughts and actions.

- "You" messages are perceived as blaming and lead to defensive feelings and actions.
- Consistently using the pronoun "I" when referring to personal feelings and thoughts obligates each of us to more accurately analyze and describe how we really feel and what we think. It helps us own the statements that we make.
- As we become more accustomed to and comfortable with labeling our feelings and thoughts with "I feel" or "I think" statements, we rely less on "you" messages. The proper use of the "I" message produces clearer, more succinct, and effective communication.
- The effective "I" message has three parts:

  - A nonblaming, nonjudgmental description of the perceived problem (*"When telephone messages are not delivered to me promptly . . ."*)
  - A description of the tangible or concrete effect that the perceived problem has on me (*". . . then I cannot return the calls in a timely fashion."*)
  - A description of the specific feelings generated within the person who perceives the problem (*". . . and I worry that I will appear to be irresponsible and that my performance rating will suffer."*)

- Of course, the "I" message is dependent upon the relationship between the sender and the receiver. If the relationship is positive, then, using the example above, the receiver is more apt to alter her or his behavior. If the relationship is negative or nonexistent, the receiver may respond with "Who cares?" The "I" message is not a magic bullet that will cure all ills of poor communication; however, it is another tool that you can apply in appropriate circumstances.

Communicating with "E"-mail: "E"fficient? Probably; "E"ffective? Not necessarily

Just because we have the capability of doing something, that does not obligate us to act upon it. We have choices; we decide when, where, how, and with whom to do different things.

So it is with e-mail. As harried administrators face increased demands to do more in the same or seemingly less time, and given the convenience of electronic communication, it is tempting to try to save time and energy (and in some cases, avoid face-to-face confrontation) by communicating via the keyboard. However, doing so only addresses one-half of the communication equation, which is the sending, or encoding, segment. The other, and equally important, part of communication is the receiving, or decoding, segment. For all of its efficiency, e-mail fails to convey the nuances of face-to-face conversation; remember that the "e" in e-mail does *not* stand for "emote."

Misinterpretations of e-mail messages are commonplace. A brief "sorry about that" e-mail apology is not likely to be as well received as one that is delivered in person. An e-mail note of congratulations accompanied with a profusion of colors, bells, and whistles pales when compared to a personal conversation that combines eye contact, a warm smile, and a handshake or pat on the back. Staff members may perceive a form-letter type of e-mail message—which the principal constructed simply as a friendly, well-intentioned reminder about performing some routine act of responsibility—as a cold, stern, disapproving reprimand, because the receivers did not have the opportunity to hear the tone of voice or to see the facial expressions and body language of the sender.

Am I suggesting that you not use e-mail? No, e-mail is a wonderful communication tool. However, I am encouraging you to make conscious decisions about when to use e-mail. When you decide to communicate via e-mail, employ positive interpersonal communication techniques. For example, when possible, personalize your messages with the use of the receiver's name and include some reference to the receiver's well-being. Inject humor where appropriate, perhaps underscoring your intended jocularity with a clear "hah!" or inserting the commonly recognized "smiley face" to convey a pleasant tone.

In responding to messages received, show that you care about the other person and her or his message by responding promptly. Demonstrate active listening just as you might in person-to-person conversation—ask clarifying questions and paraphrase the message sent by the other person to make sure you understand the meaning.

Improve your communication—remember how to get to Carnegie Hall

The story goes like this: Seeking directions to reach Carnegie Hall, a young musician, carrying a violin case, stopped another pedestrian on a sidewalk in New York City and said: "Excuse me. Could you tell me how to get to Carnegie Hall?" The other man looked at the violin case and then responded in an all-knowing tone, "Certainly. To get to Carnegie Hall, young man, you must practice, practice, practice!"

The same is true about developing effective communication. We must consistently practice positive communication skills such as active listening and "I" messages, so that those skills become a matter of habit—a natural part of our being.

RECOMMENDED READINGS RELATED TO "DECIPHERING THE JOB"

This third section of *The Portable Mentor* analyzed and interpreted the job of the school principal. Expressed another way, it offered ideas about what sense we make of the job and what sense we make of ourselves—what have we learned? It also acknowledged the centrality of communication to the success of the principal. The following recommended readings parallel this message.

Practicing and promoting good communication in the workplace is the theme of the Adler and Elmhorst text, while Kegan and Lahey stress the power of mental language and its effect upon each of us. Dyer and Carothers link communication with our intuitive powers, while Covey describes habits that enable our behaviors to be more effective. Blanchard and Johnson use the life and times of some small creatures to offer a powerful parable about the relationship between change and our attitudes and expectations.

* * *

Adler, R. B., & Elmhorst, J. (1996). *Communicating at Work: Principles and Practices for Business and the Professions.* New York: McGraw-Hill.

Blanchard, K. H., & Johnson, S. (1998). *Who Moved My Cheese?—An Amazing Way to Deal With Change in Your Work and in Your Life.* East Rutherford, NJ: Putnam.

Covey, S. R. (1989). *The 7 Habits of Highly Effective People.* New York: Simon & Schuster.

Dyer, K. M., & Carothers, J. (2000). *The Intuitive Principal: A Guide to Leadership.* Thousand Oaks, CA: Corwin.

Kegan, R., & Lahey, L. L. (2001). *How the Way We Talk Can Change the Way We Work.* San Francisco: Jossey-Bass.

Owen, H. (1997). *Open Space Technology: A User's Guide.* San Francisco: Berrett-Koehler.

PART IV

Mentoring the Mentor

Determine Expectations 23

In the preceding parts of this book, I served as an "on-paper" mentor for the entry-year principal. In this fourth part, I am switching roles; here I take on the task of being the "on-paper" mentor for the principal-mentor—hence the title of this section, "Mentoring the Mentor." I encourage the entry-year principal to continue reading this section and "listen in," because the information offered to the beginning principal-mentor also benefits the beginning principal.

As a first-time principal-mentor, where and how do you start? And what are you to do as a mentor? My overview of an effective approach to mentoring a first-year principal includes the following five areas:

1. Determine expectations (see below).

2. Build the relationship between you and your mentee.

3. Help your mentee survive on the job.

4. Help your mentee improve on the job.

5. Help your mentee grow professionally.

Modules 23 to 27 provide more details about these responsibilities.

Before you begin any mentoring activities, it is essential that you understand what your employer expects of you as a principal-mentor. If the employer has not specified expectations for you, I suggest that you request such information. The school district leadership, in the person of your supervisor, should have a written agreement with you about the following issues:

- Participation of the mentee: Is the entry-year principal required to participate in the mentoring program, or is it a matter of personal choice?
- Time: How long is the formal mentor-mentee relationship to last, that is, is this arrangement limited to the mentee's first year? How frequently are you to meet with your mentee?

- Compensation: Will you be compensated, and if so, how?
- Authority and evaluation: (Special note: Your relationship with your mentee will be stronger because the trust level will be stronger, if the answer to each of the following questions is "no.") Does the school district administration expect you to monitor and control the actions of the mentee? Are you accountable for the mentee's performance? Are you to participate in the formal evaluation of the mentee?
- It is advisable to determine if the school district leadership has informed the mentee of the expectations that the district holds for you and for the mentee. If the district has not informed your mentee of such expectations, verify that this will take place before you initiate contact.

In addition to knowing what your employer expects of you, it is important that you know what you expect of yourself as a principal-mentor. I urge you to reflect on your goals for serving as a mentor; record them early in the mentoring process, refer to them on a regular basis, and use them for evaluating your growth as a mentor.

It is also important to clarify the expectations of your mentee. This is not something you would do the first time that you meet; however, it should occur early in your relationship. Gaining an understanding of the mentee's expectations could be as simple as engaging him or her in a conversation about the services she or he expects of you. While that approach is congenial, it can be rather one-sided. A more enriching experience occurs when you and your mentee mutually establish an understanding of your role. The two of you can seek consensus regarding the services the mentee desires from you and the services you are willing and able to deliver. An example of a form that you and your mentee can use to clarify expectations appears in Table 13.

Table 13

Mentor Services Expectation Sheet		
Directions: Some mentees and mentors may choose to discuss and complete this sheet in one setting. Others may prefer to complete Stages 1 and 2 separately and then meet (Stage 3) to seek consensus. The mentee initiates one of these sheets for each focus area she or he identifies.		
Stage 1:	Stage 2:	Stage 3:
Mentee completes this column prior to submitting the sheet to the mentor	Mentor reviews items listed by the mentee, completes this column with clarifying questions and ideas for responding	Mentor and mentee review notes from Stages 1 and 2; then seek and record consensus statements below
Focus Area: What service does the mentee need or seek?	Focus Area:	Focus Area:
Rationale: Why does the mentee need or seek this service?	Rationale:	Rationale:
Delivery Strategies: How would the mentee prefer the service delivered?	Delivery Strategies:	Delivery Strategies:
Indicator(s) of Success: What will indicate that the mentor delivered the services successfully?	Indicator(s) of Success:	Indicator(s) of Success:

24 Build and Maintain the Mentoring Relationship

Your absolute, number one priority as a mentor is to initiate, foster, and sustain a relationship between you and your mentee. Without a harmonious relationship, you and your mentee will have limited communication, and when conversations do occur, they are apt to be less meaningful. It is essential that both of you feel comfortable with each other. Yes, it takes two people to make a relationship, and you are not singularly responsible for the feeling that develops between you and your mentee. However, as indicated in the following list, there are things you can do to display your desire that the two of you develop a positive and productive affiliation.

• Make the first move in becoming acquainted. Contact and introduce yourself to your mentee; begin with a telephone call and schedule an appointment to meet in person; acknowledge the mentee's schedule and your willingness to work around it. Express enthusiasm about the opportunity to serve as a principal-mentor and offer to help as needed.

• Exchange contact information—telephone numbers, including extension numbers if applicable, and e-mail addresses. Discuss "best times" to call.

• Communicate frequently; do not wait for the mentee to call for help. Beginning principals often think they must prove their mettle by solving everything in isolation, without assistance.

• Verbally share a *brief* biographical sketch of yourself, as a demonstration of openness and as a model of the kind of information you would welcome from the mentee.

• As you gather information from or about your mentee, create a file that helps you remember and acknowledge the humanness of your mentee. For example, items might include names of your mentee's family members, hometown, birthday, hobbies, and personal interests.

• Demonstrate desirable administrative traits; honor appointments, return calls or e-mail messages promptly, be organized, be professional, and be human; display a sense of humor and humility.

• Express the value you place on confidentiality, promise confidentiality, and demonstrate confidentiality.

• Share experiences with discretion; do not use the mentoring experience to boast of your exploits; mentoring is about helping the mentee grow in competence and confidence.

• Speak of mutual benefits derived from your mentoring relationship; assure your mentee that you value lifelong learning and that you expect to gain from this experience.

• Speak of your desire to help the mentee and demonstrate that desire by producing results; for example, locate and offer resource materials and contact information for resource people in a timely manner.

• Be sensitive to the power of the meeting location; offer to meet at the mentee's school—ask for a tour of the building; offer to meet off campus. Seek the preference of the mentee.

• Be sensitive to the power of "breaking bread together"; offer to meet where food is available.

• In your meetings with your mentee, model good communication techniques—make and maintain eye contact, be an "active" listener, use "I" messages when appropriate, ask clarifying questions, and be empathetic.

• Make yourself quietly available to the mentee; learn to be an "opportunistic resource." Sometimes, just by "being there," listening, posing reflective questions, and waiting patiently for the mentee to fill in the lulls in the conversation, you can elicit the undercurrent issues that otherwise might go unexpressed. Simply by being in the same room or at the other end of the phone line and allowing time for the mentee to reflect, you increase the likelihood that your mentee will offer commentary beyond the initial, "Oh, everything is just great!"

25 Help Your Mentee Survive on the Job

As you develop the all-important relationship with your mentee, you must simultaneously help the beginning principal survive the first year. I do not use the word "survive" in a minimal sense. This is not about job protection; this is not about helping the entry-year principal avoid responsibilities or escape the consequences of a sub-par performance. This is about helping the beginning principal be successful, to anticipate and plan for the successful accomplishment of duties—which is exactly why I developed the task list that appears in the "Doing the Job" part of this book.

The beginning principal, even with limited experience, can, on her or his own initiative, use the task lists provided in this manual to prepare for the basic demands of the job. You, on the other hand, with your wealth of experience, can embellish upon and refine the lists and thus guide your mentee through the maze of smaller details that helps keep the principal's ship afloat and on course. Consequently, I encourage you to schedule one session per month with your mentee, specifically for the purpose of reviewing the tasks associated with the ensuing month. Then you can help your mentee evaluate her or his preparation for those upcoming tasks. I created the following "Mentor-Mentee Discussion Guide" (see Table 14) to facilitate such discussion sessions.

The opportunity for you to help your mentee cope with problematic issues depends on the willingness of your mentee to confide in you, which in turn depends on the trust level that exists between the two of you. Initially, you may find that your mentee is reluctant to express a need for assistance. Some principals (not just those in their first year) think they must resolve all issues on their own. This could be due to a number of reasons—personal ego, a desire to project competence, or a fear of receiving a poor evaluation. As the trust level builds between the two of you, however, so too will the mentee turn to you increasingly for assistance.

Table 14

MODULE 25: **129**
HELP YOUR
MENTEE SURVIVE
ON THE JOB

Mentor-Mentee Discussion Guide

Prior to a scheduled meeting, mentor and mentee each use this sheet to record notes regarding items for discussion.

MENTOR NOTES	**MENTEE NOTES**
1. Discussion items for our meeting on: [Date] _____	1. Discussion items for our meeting on: [Date] _____
2. Looking Ahead: • Reviewing the tasks and time frame listed in *The Portable Mentor*. • Other:	2. Looking Ahead: • Reviewing the tasks and time frame listed in *The Portable Mentor*. • Other:
3. Agreed-upon action steps to be taken by the mentor before the next meeting:	3. Agreed-upon action steps to be taken by the mentee before the next meeting:

Next Meeting:

Date: _____ Time: _____ Location: _____

When your mentee hints at, or openly expresses, a concern, issue, or problem, or when you suspect or detect that such a condition might exist, encourage your mentee to talk about it. Keep in mind that *the mentoring process is about the mentee, not the mentor*. Yes, you will learn and grow from the mentoring experience, but your number one responsibility as a mentor is to help the *mentee* learn and grow, to help the *mentee* become more confident and self-sufficient. To assist your mentee with some troubling incident, consider using a reflective process such as the one illustrated in Table 15.

Table 15

<u>A Reflective Process for Responding
to a Mentee's Search for a Solution</u>

1. Ask the mentee to elaborate on her or his perception of the situation.

2. Actively listen and reflect the emotions being expressed by the mentee.

3. Ask clarifying questions; identify the pertinent information.

4. Summarize your understanding of the situation; that is, verify the mentee's perception of the situation.

5. Ask "thought-provoking" questions; for example, Have you considered . . . ? Could you try . . . ? What do you think might happen if you . . . ?

6. Engage the mentee in generating viable alternatives.

7. Engage the mentee in ranking the alternatives.

8. Encourage the mentee to choose a course of action.

9. Help the mentee establish an appropriate order of action steps and related timeframe.

10. Make notes to remind you to revisit this issue in a follow-up conversation with your mentee.

Help Your Mentee Improve on the Job

26

In this module, I will operate on two assumptions—that you and your mentee have established an effective relationship and that your mentee is successfully surviving on the job. Given this presumption of success, I want to direct your attention to the higher-level goal of encouraging your mentee to *think about* improving his or her performance in a systematic and ongoing manner, that is, developing as a professional educator. This can be very challenging, for both the entry-year principal and for you! The beginning principal has so much to assimilate during the first year that you must be very judicious in guiding your mentee toward attempting self-improvement ventures. That is why I emphasize encouraging your mentee to *think about* improving. Realizing that the need to expand one's horizons is critical, especially early in one's career, my recommended strategy is one of planting the seeds of self-improvement during the entry year, thus exposing your mentee to a larger picture of what school leadership can be. Unless exposed to a conceptual framework that encompasses the totality of the principalship, a beginning principal can acquire a narrow, and long-lasting, perspective of the job. The day-to-day pressures of solving emergencies can take precedence over the more significant, "big-picture" leadership issues.

How can you expose your mentee to the larger picture of what the model principalship entails? I recommend that you use the framework of ISLLC Standards, which are both comprehensive and widely accepted. The ISSLC Standards, with detailed indicator statements that describe the knowledge, dispositions, and performances of effective school leaders, provide a circumspective summary of the principalship. The following statement from the Council of Chief State School Officers Web site reflects the widespread acceptance of the Standards: "Thirty-five states have either adopted or adapted the ISLLC Standards and are in different stages of implementing the Standards in reforming educational leadership within their state" (CCSSO, 1996).

Nonetheless, while the ISLLC Standards provide a valid framework for analyzing the principalship, few first-year principals have the time, energy, or desire to engage in a detailed discussion about applying these Standards to their jobs. Most first-year principals will resist spending time on activities that they perceive as theoretical, in favor of what they know to be real—their work world. Therefore, to involve the entry-year principal in thinking about the larger picture—to move your mentee toward self-improvement—I urge you to engage your mentee in a discussion about situations in her or his workplace that relate to the Standards. In other words, connect the mentee's real-life, day-to-day experiences to the seemingly less concrete, conceptual model.

How do you spark such discussion with your mentee? One way is to solicit examples of such connections from the mentee. However, the beginning principal may not initially recognize the relationship between the work-related events and the ISLLC Standards. To facilitate meaningful conversation with entry-year principals regarding the linking of day-to-day school events and the ISLLC Standards, I created a series of 22 scenarios, which appears in the following module. I encourage you to investigate the use of these scenarios with your mentee.

Promote Your Mentee's Professional Growth Through ISLLC-Based Scenarios **27**

Given your experience, I trust that you will find that many, if not all, of the following scenarios are familiar—perhaps painfully or comically so. The scenarios are reality-based and serve as productive conversation starters. I suggest that before you engage your mentee in a discussion of the scenarios, you review all 22 of them to become familiar with their content and the suggested discussion prompts. Initially, given what you know about your mentee and her or his situation, select a scenario that you think will have the most relevance to your mentee. Introduce the scenario with a low-key approach; allow sufficient time for your mentee to read and reflect on the scenario before engaging her or him in any discussion. Over time, introduce and discuss scenarios from all six ISLLC Standards. Your goal is to help your mentee recognize the connection between the real and the conceptual. In this way, you can show your mentee that the ISLLC Standards provide a realistic framework for conceptualizing the role of the principal; hence all six of the Standards take on a validity that can broaden your mentee's perception of the principal's role. Tables 16 through 21 will help you connect the 22 scenarios with the ISLLC Standards they reflect.

The 22 scenarios on the following pages are presented in the form of memos, letters, and telephone and e-mail messages; these communiqués simulate situations that a principal might encounter on the job. The strategy for using them involves the following steps:

Table 16

This table illustrates the correlation between the ISLLC Standard 1 and scenarios 01 through 04.			
ISLLC Standard:		**Scenarios:**	
No.	Description	No.	Description
1	" . . . facilitating the development, articulation, implementation, and stewardship of a *vision of learning* that is shared and supported by the school community."	01	Assistant Superintendent Ivan E. Goe poses questions for the principals as the district embarks on a review of each school's vision and mission statements.
		02	Supt. DeMann asks the principals how the schools will communicate vision & mission statements.
		03	An anonymous student questions the propriety of another student (Marsha Laww) conducting a survey that measures whether students, teachers, parents, and other citizens actually know the school's vision & mission statements.
		04	Ray Gunn, president of the teachers' union, questions how the school district will pay for the implementation of the revised vision & mission statements.

1. Select a scenario for you and your mentee to discuss.

2. Give a copy of the selected scenario to your mentee.

3. After allowing time for your mentee to read the scenario, engage her or him in a discussion of the issues associated with the scenario (suggested discussion questions accompany each scenario).

MODULE 27: **135**
PROMOTE
YOUR MENTEE'S
PROFESSIONAL
GROWTH
THROUGH
ISLLC-BASED
SCENARIOS

Table 17

This table illustrates the correlation between the ISLLC Standard 2 and scenarios 05 through 08.			
ISLLC Standard:		**Scenarios:**	
No.	Description	No.	Description
2	" . . . advocating, nurturing, and sustaining a *school culture* and *instructional program* conducive to student learning and staff professional growth."	05	R. T. Phactt, resident of a local retirement home, asks the principal to explain the low performance of Urrtown students on state tests.
		06	Perry Patettic asks if and how teachers match their choices of instructional methodologies with the different learning styles and needs of students.
		07	Eunice Eichel perceives a lack of recognition for students' achievements outside the school and questions the school's value for the culture of the community.
		08	Van Ishing shares his concern that a teacher fails to accommodate students' different strengths when evaluating student performance.

4. The next-to-last discussion question asks your mentee to identify the ISLLC Standards most closely associated with the scenario (you may need to provide a copy of the six ISLLC Standards). Over time, your mentee will likely realize that many, if not all, job-related situations represent an integration of several Standards.

5. The final discussion question focuses on the kind of documentation and artifacts that are likely to surface during the resolution of the scenario. Responding to this question helps the mentee develop a habit of discerning "evidence of leadership" documentation (in the form of artifacts) that she or he can collect as, or after, the problem is resolved.

Table 18

This table illustrates the correlation between the ISLLC Standard 3 and scenarios 09 through 12.			
ISLLC Standards:		**Scenarios:**	
No.	Description	No.	Description
3	"... ensuring *management* of the organization, operations, and resources for a safe, efficient, and effective learning environment."	09	Mollie Koddle questions the school's safety and raises concerns about the care and cleanliness of the physical plant.
		10	Ray Gunn relays some concerns of teachers regarding the techniques employed by the administration to achieve the timely identification and resolution of potential problems and the methods used for conflict resolution.
		11	Anne Tippathee asks how taxpayers who do not have children enrolled in the schools are to participate in decisions that have a community impact.
		12	Phil Langees questions if and how teachers stay current with research.

MODULE 27: **137**
PROMOTE
YOUR MENTEE'S
PROFESSIONAL
GROWTH
THROUGH
ISLLC-BASED
SCENARIOS

Table 19

This table illustrates the correlation between the ISLLC Standard 4 and scenarios 13 through 16.			
ISLLC Standards:		**Scenarios:**	
No.	Description	No.	Description
4	"... *collaborating* with *families* and *community* members, responding to diverse *community* interests and needs, and mobilizing *community* resources."	13	Rev. Mel N. Colley feels schools do not value the diversity of the community.
		14	Marshall Laww, a potential candidate for the upcoming school board election, asserts that the schools ignore diversity and intentionally exclude groups and individuals that express differing opinions.
		15	Mort U. Errey seeks information about school-community partnerships.
		16	Supt. DeMann asks the district principals to explain how they achieve and maintain visibility in the community.

Table 20

This table illustrates the correlation between the ISLLC Standard 5 and scenarios 17 through 19.			
ISLLC Standards:		**Scenarios:**	
No.	Description	No.	Description
5	" . . . acting with *integrity, fairness*, and in an *ethical manner*."	17	Grant A. Woosh seeks information regarding the methods that principals use to inspire other school employees to higher levels of performance.
		18	Mary Whey offers cost-free condominium vacation.
		19	Phil Langees announces plans for members of his community group, CHAOS, to visit the schools so that they can assess their effectiveness and issue a report to the community.

Table 21

MODULE 27: **139**
PROMOTE
YOUR MENTEE'S
PROFESSIONAL
GROWTH
THROUGH
ISLLC-BASED
SCENARIOS

This table illustrates the correlation between the ISLLC Standard 6 and scenarios 20 through 22.			
ISLLC Standards:		**Scenarios:**	
No.	Description	No.	Description
6	" . . . understanding, responding to, and influencing the *larger political, economic, legal,* and *cultural context.*"	20	Neal Downe relays a rumor about new construction in the school district and the probable influx of non-English-speaking immigrant families.
		21	Sandy Beech seeks an interview regarding the nature and degree of cooperation between school leaders and those officials who create and monitor school-related laws and regulations.
		22	Roy Al Payne challenges the "palsy-walsy" relationship that he perceives between school leaders and politicians.

Scenario 01

URRTOWN SCHOOL DISTRICT
DEPARTMENT OF CURRICULUM AND SUPERVISION

Mr. Ivan E. Goe, Assistant Superintendent

TO: All principals
RE: Vision and mission statements for each school

As you will recall from our most recent Administrative Council meeting, the superintendent has charged me with the responsibility of revising or establishing vision and mission statements for each school in the district. Given the enormity of my schedule, I must rely on the capable leadership of each building administrator to assure that this extremely important project moves forward in a timely and efficient manner.

As a preliminary step in achieving successful completion of this assignment, I am asking that each principal prepare and forward to me a detailed plan for either revising an existing vision and mission statement or developing them for the first time.

In your plan, please indicate the following:

- Whom will you involve in writing or rewriting your building's vision and mission statements?
- Specify objectives and strategies for achieving the vision and mission after the statements are written or rewritten.
- What data will you use to write or rewrite the vision and mission statements? For example, will you use data regarding student assessment and demographics of the students, their families, and the community? If so, clarify your source for such data. Describe how the vision and mission statements will be regularly monitored, evaluated, and revised in the future.

As always, I stand ready to assist you. Do not hesitate to contact me for direction.

MODULE 27: **141**
PROMOTE
YOUR MENTEE'S
PROFESSIONAL
GROWTH
THROUGH
ISLLC-BASED
SCENARIOS

Discussion Prompts Related to the Memo From Ivan E. Goe

1. As the principal, would you respond to this memo? Explain your answer.

2. If you choose to respond, how would you respond—in writing, by telephone, in person, or through a designee—and when would you respond?

3. Would you seek additional information before responding? If "yes," what additional information would you seek?

4. If you seek information from others, do you foresee any risks to your career or reputation in doing so? Should a first-year principal attempt to resolve issues such as those presented in this scenario without seeking help from others? Explain your answer.

5. If you foresee issues in this scenario that might develop into future pitfalls, please identify them. How do you interpret Ivan E. Goe's use of the phrase, "Given the enormity of my schedule"? Do you see any inconsistencies in Mr. Goe's message? (Hint: see his final two sentences.) Will your interpretation of these remarks influence your interactions with Mr. Goe and if "yes," how?

6. This scenario relates to ISLLC Standard 1. If you see a connection between this scenario and other ISLLC Standards, please explain the connection.

7. What artifacts might you collect as, or after, you resolve the situation depicted in the scenario that would serve as evidence of your leadership?

Scenario 02

URRTOWN SCHOOL DISTRICT
OFFICE OF THE SUPERINTENDENT

Mr. I. B. DeMann, Superintendent

TO: All principals
RE: Vision and mission statements

As a follow-up to the recent meeting of our Administrative Council, during which I announced that Assistant Superintendent Goe would direct and coordinate the work related to writing or rewriting vision and mission statements for each school, I want to challenge the leadership abilities of our building administrators just a bit. I realize this project is just getting started and that we are a couple of months away from completing this vital task; however, please indulge me as I look to the future.

Here is my question: Once we have the vision and mission statements in place, how do we communicate them to others? Please take a few moments to jot down (and forward to me) some ideas you think you ought to consider when you start communicating your school's vision and mission statements to others.

In addition, please do not interpret the word "communicating" as being limited to the printed word. Think outside of the box! What can you do to demonstrate the vision and mission statements to others?

I am confident that—together—we can accomplish much!

—IBD

MODULE 27: **143**
PROMOTE
YOUR MENTEE'S
PROFESSIONAL
GROWTH
THROUGH
ISLLC-BASED
SCENARIOS

Discussion Prompts Related to the Memo From I. B. DeMann

1. As the principal, would you respond to this letter? Explain your answer.

2. If you choose to respond, how would you respond—in writing, by telephone, in person, or through a designee—and when would you respond?

3. Would you seek additional information before responding? If "yes," what additional information would you seek?

4. Does this memo from the superintendent introduce an element of competition between building-level administrators? If "yes," what are the implications for you? If "no," explain your answer.

5. If you foresee issues in this scenario that might develop into future pitfalls, please identify them. For example, what do you make of Superintendent DeMann's seemingly casual directive that you "jot down (and forward to me) some ideas"? (Remember, the person that he indicated in the opening paragraph of this memo would "direct and coordinate . . . ")

6. This scenario relates to ISLLC Standard 1. If you see a connection between this scenario and other ISLLC Standards, please explain the connection.

7. What artifacts might you collect as, or after, you resolve the situation depicted in the scenario that would serve as evidence of your leadership?

Scenario 03

Dear Principal,

Is it OK if Marsha Laww conducts a survey for her father about our school <u>during</u> school time? Can't she get into some big trouble for doing that? Please say she WILL, get in trouble! She acts so special, like ... she thinks she is so-o-o hot just because her dad, Marshall, is going to run for the School Board next year. You'd think he had already won to hear her shoot off her mouth! She's always going on, "When my Daddy is on the board, we will get things done <u>our way</u> and we're going to get rid of some of the loser teachers in this school." Anyway, lately Marsha is like going around asking different people if they know what the school's mission statement is and if they know about the school's vision statement. Yeah, right! Like, who would even know that stuff? Now, you know her dad put her up to that! No way does she know anything about that stuff on her own. Oh, yeah, and another thing she does is crack on the teachers all the time cause so few of them can answer her stupid questions about mission and vision statements. And of course, none of us kids do. She even asked some of the parents at different ball games and concerts. She said the parents didn't do much better than anyone else on her stupid survey.

I hope you will check into this, even if I don't sign my name. Me and Billy Jean don't want to get into trouble, but we sure hope Marsha Laww does!!!

MODULE 27: **145**
PROMOTE
YOUR MENTEE'S
PROFESSIONAL
GROWTH
THROUGH
ISLLC-BASED
SCENARIOS

Discussion Prompts Related
to the Letter From an Anonymous Student

1. As the principal, would you respond to this letter? Explain your answer.

2. If you choose to respond, how would you respond—in writing, by telephone, in person, or through a designee—and when would you respond?

3. Would you seek additional information before responding? If "yes," what additional information would you seek?

4. If you foresee issues in this scenario that might develop into future pitfalls, please identify them. For example, if you identify the student who authored this letter, do you talk with that student? Given the apparent animosity between this student and Marsha Laww, do you get involved in it? What if you do nothing and a larger problem develops? Is there a larger issue at work here? Have the apparent results of Marsha Laww's alleged survey revealed anything that warrants your attention?

5. What about future anonymous communiqués (written or telephoned) that you may receive? How do you respond to them?

6. This scenario relates to ISLLC Standard 1. If you see a connection between this scenario and other ISLLC Standards, please explain the connection.

7. What artifacts might you collect as, or after, you resolve the situation depicted in the scenario that would serve as evidence of your leadership?

Scenario 04

URRTOWN CLASSROOM TEACHERS ASSOCIATION

Ray Gunn, President

TO: All Urrtown building administrators

RE: Resources for implementing the district's mission and goals

I wish to commend the administration for the leadership it has recently demonstrated by pursuing the writing or rewriting of mission and vision statements for each of building in the school district. The membership of Urrtown Classroom Teachers Association stands ready to assist in this creative venture.

No doubt, additional projects or work-related tasks will arise from the statements that are generated. Summarily, additional costs will result. Therefore, UCTA must question the district's preparedness to appropriately and effectively *implement* such mission and vision statements once the writing phase is concluded.

I must, in my capacity as official spokesperson for the teaching ranks, raise the bottom-line question: How does the school district intend to seek and secure the support that is necessary to implement these newly designed statements of vision and mission?

Please advise me of your response to this critical question so that I can assure the UCTA membership that monies will not be diverted from existing or future teacher-compensation funds.

MODULE 27: **147**
PROMOTE
YOUR MENTEE'S
PROFESSIONAL
GROWTH
THROUGH
ISLLC-BASED
SCENARIOS

Discussion Prompts Related to the Memo From Ray Gunn

1. As the principal, would you respond to this letter? Explain your answer.

2. If you choose to respond, how would you respond—in writing, by telephone, in person, or through a designee—and when would you respond?

3. Would you seek additional information before responding? If "yes," what additional information would you seek?

4. Would you seek the assistance of the teachers' union as offered in the first paragraph of Ray Gunn's memo? If "yes," what sort of assistance would you seek? If "no," why would you not seek it?

5. Would you expect there to be additional implementation costs and increased need for support as predicted by Ray Gunn? If you disagree with Mr. Gunn, explain your rationale. If you agree with the union president, what might those additional costs and needs be? How might such additional costs and needs affect the operation of the school that you serve?

6. If you foresee issues in this scenario that might develop into future pitfalls, please identify them.

7. This scenario relates to ISLLC Standard 1. If you see a connection between this scenario and other ISLLC Standards, please explain the connection.

8. What artifacts might you collect as, or after, you resolve the situation depicted in the scenario that would serve as evidence of your leadership?

Scenario 05

Shady Acres Retirement Village
86 Rockaby Lane
Urrtown, Urrstate

Dear Principal,

My job as president of the Shady Acres Retirement Village Entertainment Committee is to arrange for speakers to come talk to us about different stuff. Last night, some of us "youngsters" (we call ourselves youngsters because most of the other residents here are much older than we are) were sitting around talking about past times and the subject of school came up. According to the TV and the local newspaper, Urrtown students struggle with the state tests. So, we were wondering if you would come tell us why this is so. Why can't Urrtown students score higher? Are there things that block our kids from doing better? If there are, please explain what they are and what you are doing about them. We worry that the resale value of properties we own will go down like the test scores. And we pay taxes, too, you know! My buddy, Dewey Fields, still pays on his apartment building over on Park Place, for example, and Eileen Dover owns that big house that her kids live in, and she says they refuse to give her a cent for her property taxes!

Oh, yes, and we also vote, every Election Day! The voting precinct is right here in our General Meeting room. So, you should pay attention to us even if we do have to live here in this retirement home. Let me know a good time for you to come speak to us (most any day is good for us as long as it is after "The Price Is Right" and before "Wheel of Fortune"). Please send me some notes of what you will be talking about, so I can let some of the older residents know. They need time to think about stuff that is going on nowadays. Thank you.

—*R. T. Phactt*

MODULE 27: **149**
PROMOTE
YOUR MENTEE'S
PROFESSIONAL
GROWTH
THROUGH
ISLLC-BASED
SCENARIOS

Discussion Prompts Related
to the Letter From R. T. Phactt

1. As the principal, would you respond to this letter? Explain your answer.

2. If you choose to respond, how would you respond—in writing, by telephone, in person, or through a designee—and when would you respond?

3. Would you seek additional information before responding? If "yes," what additional information would you seek?

4. What approach would you take, if you agree to speak to the residents of the Shady Acres Retirement Village? What issues should you be prepared to address? Would you go as the only speaker, or would you include other school representatives—and if you would include others, who would you include, and why?

5. If you foresee issues in this scenario that might develop into future pitfalls, please identify them. (Hint: you may encounter some value clashes because of different generational experiences.)

6. This scenario relates to ISLLC Standard 2. If you see a connection between this scenario and other ISLLC Standards, please explain the connection.

7. What artifacts might you collect as, or after, you resolve the situation depicted in the scenario that would serve as evidence of your leadership?

Scenario 06

The Global Gallivanting Group
"Customized Travels for Nomadic Novices"
Perry Patettic, President and CEO

Dear Principal:

Having enjoyed a successful business in the field of world travel for over two decades, I am now ready to leave the helter-skelter pace of the metropolitan lifestyle and return to my roots. As a graduate of Urrtown High School and Urrtown University with six school-age children, I appreciate the importance of having my children attend schools that provide meaningful learning experiences. I plan to purchase a home in your school's attendance area and enroll three of my children in your building. Each of my children has distinct learning strengths and needs. Please help me assess whether the curricular offerings and instructional patterns at your school will accommodate the learning styles of each child. My good friend, Ivan E. Goe, directed me to call you for an appointment when you and I can meet. I expect that you will be able to provide me with specific examples of how your school provides the following:

1. How do your teachers provide multiple learning opportunities for students?

2. Do your teachers use multiple sources of information to assess student performance?

3. How do your teachers use technology?

4. How do you and your staff assure that there is a high level of expectation for students and staff?

5. How do you supervise and evaluate your teachers; that is, how do you hold staff members accountable for student success?

I will call soon. I look forward to meeting with you and becoming more familiar with the learning opportunities that are available for the students at your school.

—*Perry Patettic*

MODULE 27: **151**
PROMOTE
YOUR MENTEE'S
PROFESSIONAL
GROWTH
THROUGH
ISLLC-BASED
SCENARIOS

Discussion Prompts Related to the Letter From Perry Patettic

1. As the principal, would you respond to this letter? Explain your answer.

2. If you choose to respond, how would you respond—in writing, by telephone, in person, or through a designee—and when would you respond?

3. Would you seek additional information before responding? If "yes," what additional information would you seek?

4. How do you interpret the phrase, "My good friend, Ivan E. Goe, directed me to call you for an appointment when you and I can meet."? If you determine this to be true, would you have expected Ivan E. Goe to tell you in advance? If it proven true and Mr. Goe did not tell you in advance, what action do you take toward Mr. Goe, if any? Do you have any concern that Perry Patettic may be a "name dropper"?

5. If you foresee issues in this scenario that might develop into future pitfalls, please identify them.

6. This scenario relates to ISLLC Standard 2. If you see a connection between this scenario and other ISLLC Standards, please explain the connection.

7. What artifacts might you collect as, or after, you resolve the situation depicted in the scenario that would serve as evidence of your leadership?

Scenario 07

*Eunice Eichel
6699 Revolutions Road
Urrtown, Urrstate*

To the attention of the principal:

I wish to register a concern that could very well spin its way into a complaint to the school board should you choose to not properly address it. I currently serve as the president of the Urrtown Unicycle Union, Unit No. 247, which is a certified unit of the National Unicycle Union. Recently, our local union had several members participate in the regional unicycle competition that was held in neighboring Wheelersville. One youngster, who happens to be my daughter, Tryce, won the contest for her age group. This was prominently reported in the local newspaper and on the local access cable channel.

However, not one word of recognition for her accomplishment was given to Tryce at school! Why is this so? Must a child excel exclusively in school-related events to be acknowledged for success at school? Does not the gestalt of a student's total life include the inexorable interconnectedness between school life and life beyond the four walls of a classroom? I assure you that winning the unicycle competition significantly enriched my daughter's self-esteem (until her achievement went virtually unnoticed by her schoolteachers or principal!). I suggest to you (and I am prepared to proclaim this to the Board of Education if need be) that the accomplishments of students (and staff) ought to be recognized and *celebrated* as a part of the school's *total* culture!

I am very interested in your response to my concern, which I hope to receive before the next meeting of the Board of Education.

Respectfully submitted,

Eunice Eichel, proud mother of Tryce Eichel!

MODULE 27: **153**
PROMOTE
YOUR MENTEE'S
PROFESSIONAL
GROWTH
THROUGH
ISLLC-BASED
SCENARIOS

Discussion Prompts Related to the Letter From Eunice Eichel

1. As the principal, would you respond to this letter? Explain your answer.

2. If you choose to respond, how would you respond— in writing, by telephone, in person, or through a designee—and when would you respond?

3. Would you seek additional information before responding? If "yes," what additional information would you seek?

4. How do you interpret Eunice's phrases, "not properly address it" and "I am prepared to proclaim this to the Board of Education if need be"? Would you try to discourage Eunice from contacting the board? Why or why not?

5. How do you interpret the closing of the letter that says, "I am very interested in your response to my concern, which I hope to receive before the next meeting of the Board of Education"? If you choose to ignore this remark by Eunice Eichel, would you inform anyone of your decision? If so, whom would you inform?

6. If you foresee issues in this scenario that might develop into future pitfalls, please identify them.

7. This scenario relates to ISLLC Standard 2. If you see a connection between this scenario and other ISLLC Standards, please explain the connection.

8. What artifacts might you collect as, or after, you resolve the situation depicted in the scenario that would serve as evidence of your leadership?

Scenario 08

Van Ishing
Magician Extraordinaire!
Available for Private Parties, Celebrations, and Festive Occasions
51 Sorcerers Circle — Urrtown, Urrstate

Dear Principal Urrnamehere:

I am writing to acquire your insight into a problem that I perceive regarding my son, Ison, and one of his favorite instructors, Mr. Al Kemic. On a purely emotional level, Ison has no quarrel with Mr. Kemic. Ison very much likes and respects Mr. Kemic. However, to the considerable chagrin of Ison and myself, there are student assessment issues that seem to warrant investigation and correction. I assure you that I have previously conveyed my consternation to Mr. Kemic. Unfortunately, he has chosen to disregard my protestations. Therefore, sensing that I have no recourse, I turn to you for enlightenment regarding this gloomy situation.

Overall, I am quite satisfied with the manner in which Mr. Al Kemic presents the course content to Ison and his classmates. Mr. Kemic utilizes a variety of instructional modes and materials to capture the attention and the delight of the students. Mr. Kemic permits, nay, he encourages all students to pursue the study of the course content in a number of ways. Students may study in a purely independent manner or they may choose to engage in small-group interactions. Mr. Kemic promotes study via contemporary technology as he adroitly guides his students through the rich potential of Internet resources.

However, in the area of assessing student growth or academic progress, Mr. Kemic clings to one and only one method; he refuses to use a variety of techniques. Al Kemic relies entirely and exclusively upon paper-and-pencil testing to measure what his students have learned. My son, Ison, has *never* performed well on such measurement devices. So, despite Ison's ability to verbally describe or demonstrate the considerable knowledge that he has acquired, he is limited to responding to a "true-false, fill in the blank, choose from a list" type of assessment. This, I submit, is not only inconsistent with Mr. Kemic's overall teaching methods, but it is also an unfair and arbitrary practice that is detrimental to my son and potentially other students.

I seek your assistance in making this problem disappear.

—Van Ishing

MODULE 27: **155**
PROMOTE
YOUR MENTEE'S
PROFESSIONAL
GROWTH
THROUGH
ISLLC-BASED
SCENARIOS

Discussion Prompts Related
to the Letter From Van Ishing

1. As the principal, would you respond to this letter? Explain your answer.

2. If you choose to respond, how would you respond—in writing, by telephone, in person, or through a designee—and when would you respond?

3. Would you seek additional information before responding? If "yes," what additional information would you seek?

4. Van Ishing wants this problem to "disappear." He expects you to fix the situation as he sees it. If you cannot, or choose not to, remedy this matter as quickly as he desires and in the manner that he desires, what rationale would you offer him?

5. If you foresee issues in this scenario that might develop into future pitfalls, please identify them. For example, might your resolution of this situation affect other teachers? If "yes," clarify how your handling of this matter might affect them. If "no," explain why you think your actions will not affect them.

6. This scenario relates to ISLLC Standard 2. If you see a connection between this scenario and other ISLLC Standards, please explain the connection.

7. What artifacts might you collect as, or after, you resolve the situation depicted in the scenario that would serve as evidence of your leadership?

Scenario 09

Mrs. Mollie Koddle
1313 Purity Place
Urrtown, Urrstate

Dear Principal:

You will not recognize my name, as my family only recently moved to Urrtown. My only child, Precious, is enrolling in your school for the first time. We come to Urrtown School District from an adjacent state where we lived in a community and school district similar to Urrtown. My husband, Rollie, and I were actively involved in parent advisory groups, fundraising, and school levy campaigns.

I wish to express my grave concern about safety issues in schools across our nation and to seek your reassurance that your school is adequately prepared for the type of disasters that have befallen other schools and communities. I have listed my specific concerns below, and I would appreciate equally specific answers or examples from you.

- Is your school, its equipment, and its support systems prepared to operate in a safe, efficient, and effective manner? How can I be sure? What are the indicators that your school is operating at a high level of preparedness for emergencies?
- What measures do you take to assure the year-round cleanliness (Precious will participate in advanced placement courses during the summer) and aesthetically pleasing appearance of the school?
- Do you employ up-to-date technology to manage the operation of the school? I have a degree in computer technology and I can help in this area if you desire.
- Do you have a crisis management plan ready for implementation, in case there is an emergency or threat to the school and it occupants?

I may have follow-up questions when we meet. I will call you for an appointment.

—Mollie Koddle

MODULE 27: **157**
PROMOTE
YOUR MENTEE'S
PROFESSIONAL
GROWTH
THROUGH
ISLLC-BASED
SCENARIOS

Discussion Prompts Related
to the Letter From Mollie Koddle

1. As the principal, would you respond to this letter? Explain your answer.

2. If you choose to respond, how would you respond—in writing, by telephone, in person, or through a designee—and when would you respond?

3. Would you seek additional information before responding? If "yes," what additional information would you seek?

4. What are the implications of Mollie Koddle's questions, "How can I be sure?" and "Is your school, its equipment, and its support systems prepared to operate in a safe, efficient, and effective manner?" She may be asking for more than your verbal assurance; what indicators could you cite or produce that would show the school to be the safe haven she desires?

5. How do you interpret Mollie's statement in her opening paragraph: "My husband, Rollie, and I were actively involved in parent advisory groups, fundraising, and school levy campaigns." Will this information influence how you interact with Mr. and Mrs. Koddle?

6. If you foresee issues in this scenario that might develop into future pitfalls, please identify them.

7. This scenario relates to ISLLC Standard 3. If you see a connection between this scenario and other ISLLC Standards, please explain the connection.

8. What artifacts might you collect as, or after, you resolve the situation depicted in the scenario that would serve as evidence of your leadership?

Scenario 10

URRTOWN CLASSROOM TEACHERS ASSOCIATION

Ray Gunn, President

TO: All Urrtown building administrators
RE: Administrative procedures at the building level

I am writing to alert you to the probability that some district teachers may soon initiate a grievance against you and your fellow administrators regarding certain administrative practices. It has long been my practice to contact building administrators before grievances are formally initiated in the hopes that preliminary discussion might resolve the issue(s), and thus avoid entering into the formal, sometimes lengthy, and occasionally contentious grievance process.

To that end, I am informally advising you of the teachers' concerns and giving you this opportunity to provide examples of how you provide for the following at your school:

1. In what way do you and your staff identify and resolve potential problems?

2. How do you assure that such procedures are managed in a timely manner?

3. Please identify how you use and encourage the staff to develop group-process and consensus-building skills.

4. Please identify how you use and encourage the staff to develop conflict-resolution skills.

I would appreciate your clarification of how you provide for these important administrative procedures.

MODULE 27: **159**
PROMOTE
YOUR MENTEE'S
PROFESSIONAL
GROWTH
THROUGH
ISLLC-BASED
SCENARIOS

Discussion Prompts Related to the Memo From Ray Gunn

1. As the principal, would you respond to this memo? Explain your answer.

2. If you choose to respond, how would you respond—in writing, by telephone, in person, or through a designee—and when would you respond?

3. Would you seek additional information before responding? If "yes," what additional information would you seek?

4. How do you interpret Ray Gunn's words that "some district teachers may soon initiate a grievance against you and your fellow administrators regarding certain administrative practices"? Would you consult with teachers in the building? If so, would you approach all teachers or just those whose opinions matter most to you? Would you consult other building-level or central office administrators?

5. If you foresee issues in this scenario that might develop into future pitfalls, please identify them.

6. Do you care to know why Ray Gunn wants you to "provide examples of how you provide for the following at your school"? What if you do and other district principals do not? Keep in mind that the leader of the teachers' union may wish to pit the practices of one school principal against the practices of another. What you say or do may have implications for your fellow district administrators.

7. This scenario relates to ISLLC Standard 3. If you see a connection between this scenario and other ISLLC Standards, please explain the connection.

8. What artifacts might you collect as, or after, you resolve the situation depicted in the scenario that would serve as evidence of your leadership?

Scenario 11

ANNE TIPPATHEE
999 DISSONANCE DRIVE
URRTOWN, URRSTATE

Dear Principal:

I recently read in the *Urrtown Utopian* that each school in Urrtown is engaged in a process to develop or revise vision and mission statements. The paper gave lots of ink to ballyhooing the district's efforts to involve representatives of different parent-teacher groups, different parent-advisory groups, and different parent-booster groups.

Well, that's all well and good, if you have children in school! My four children, all Urrtown graduates, have moved on to reside in other communities. I remain here, still paying property taxes on my house. What about my involvement in the operation of the schools? Am I to be excluded from participating in school-related issues, simply because I no longer have school-age children? As a property owner, I hold a stake in what happens with the schools, maybe more so than some school district administrators who don't live in the district! I care about how and what decisions are made regarding the school's operation. How are tax-paying citizens like myself to have any sense of school ownership, other than writing checks every six months to pay taxes—and your salary, among other things? Who are you accountable to?

I would greatly appreciate your response to my concerns. Since I share a property line with your school, I can easily come to school to talk with you. Let me know when you are ready to speak with me.

—*Anne Tippathee*

MODULE 27: **161**
PROMOTE
YOUR MENTEE'S
PROFESSIONAL
GROWTH
THROUGH
ISLLC-BASED
SCENARIOS

Discussion Prompts Related
to the Letter From Anne Tippathee

1. As the principal, would you respond to this letter? Explain your answer.

2. If you choose to respond, how would you respond—in writing, by telephone, in person, or through a designee—and when would you respond?

3. Would you seek additional information before responding? If "yes," what additional information would you seek?

4. Developing an ability to "read" other people is an important skill for school administrators. Describe your interpretation of the mood projected by Anne Tippathee's letter. Do you temper your response according to Anne's likely mind-set? If so, how do you do that? Do you attach any significance to her phrase, "Since I share a property line with your school"? If so, explain how you think it might be significant.

5. If you foresee issues in this scenario that might develop into future pitfalls, please identify them.

6. This scenario relates to ISLLC Standard 3. If you see a connection between this scenario and other ISLLC Standards, please explain the connection.

7. What artifacts might you collect as, or after, you resolve the situation depicted in the scenario that would serve as evidence of your leadership?

Scenario 12

PHIL LANGEES, M.D.
Specializing in Hand Surgery Since 1996
Urrtown Medical Center
10 Metacarpal Blvd.
Urrtown, Urrstate

Dear Principal:

I recently returned from a medical research conference, which I voluntarily attended in a desire to update my skill level as a hand surgeon. Coincidentally, on my first evening back home, I found myself engaged in a conversation with my youngest child who, while complaining about the boredom he is experiencing in one of his classes, portrayed his teacher using teaching methods that I know the teacher used with my three older children. That means this individual is using the same instructional methods that he used, rather unsuccessfully I might add, some ten years ago.

As I mused over this situation, and having just returned from the "updating skills" conference, I found myself wondering about the discovery and application of research in the field of education. Is nothing new in teaching methodologies? I suspect there is. As one example, consider the wealth of information recently developed in the area of brain research. I wonder; when new trends or research findings emerge, how do teachers recognize, study, and apply such information?

In summary, I look forward to receiving your response to my questions regarding teachers' recognition, study, and application of research-based methodologies and trends.

—Phil Langees, M.D.

MODULE 27: **163**
PROMOTE
YOUR MENTEE'S
PROFESSIONAL
GROWTH
THROUGH
ISLLC-BASED
SCENARIOS

Discussion Prompts Related
to the Letter From Phil Langees

1. As the principal, would you respond to this letter? Explain your answer.

2. If you choose to respond, how would you respond—in writing, by telephone, in person, or through a designee—and when would you respond?

3. Would you seek additional information before responding? If "yes," what additional information would you seek?

4. How would you determine, for your response to the letter from Phil Langees or for your own edification, whether the teaching staff "recognizes, studies, and applies research-based methodologies and trends"? What is your role as school leader in this area?

5. If you foresee issues in this scenario that might develop into future pitfalls, please identify them.

6. This scenario relates to ISLLC Standard 3. If you see a connection between this scenario and other ISLLC Standards, please explain the connection.

7. What artifacts might you collect as, or after, you resolve the situation depicted in the scenario that would serve as evidence of your leadership?

Scenario 13

Reverend Mel N. Colley
The Church of Sainted Holy Redeemers
101 Donation Drive
Urrtown, Urrstate

Dear Principal,

It is with heavy heart that I write you this day. It grieves me deeply when I see injustices inflicted on innocent people, and yet I see such unfortunate developments stemming from the operation of your school. It seems to me, given the amount of disharmony in the world today, that you should, and could, seize the opportunity to ensure fairness for all members of the community.

Yet I see little, if any, effort on the part of your school to reach out to members of churches, clubs, political groups, or service organizations that represent the minorities present in our community. Members of these groups are decent, hard-working citizens who deserve acknowledgement. Surely, if you value diversity and richness in the fabric of your school's culture, you will find ways to reach out and structure your school's organization to be more inclusive. You must identify and nurture relationships between the school and community leaders, if we are ever to overcome the disparities in today's society.

If I am incorrect, if my judgments are themselves unjust, if my observations are oblique, then I pray that you will educate me in the errors of my perception. Please lift my spirits with examples of school programs that exist beyond my awareness. Show me how the school is collaborating with families and community members, responding to diverse community interests and needs, and mobilizing community resources. I thank you!

—*Reverend Mel N. Colley*
The Church of Sainted Holy Redeemers

MODULE 27: **165**
PROMOTE
YOUR MENTEE'S
PROFESSIONAL
GROWTH
THROUGH
ISLLC-BASED
SCENARIOS

Discussion Prompts Related
to the Letter From Mel N. Colley

1. As the principal, would you respond to this letter? Explain your answer.

2. If you choose to respond, how would you respond—in writing, by telephone, in person, or through a designee—and when would you respond?

3. Would you seek additional information before responding? If "yes," what additional information would you seek?

4. The Reverend Mel N. Colley suggests that the school is not doing enough to promote diversity, and he closes his letter with a request that you "show" him how the school is collaborating with families and community members, responding to diverse community interests and needs, and mobilizing community resources. If you choose to respond to his request, how would you "show" that the school was doing these things? What evidence would you produce?

5. If you foresee issues in this scenario that might develop into future pitfalls, please identify them.

6. This scenario relates to ISLLC Standard 4. If you see a connection between this scenario and other ISLLC Standards, please explain the connection.

7. What artifacts might you collect as, or after, you resolve the situation depicted in the scenario that would serve as evidence of your leadership?

Scenario 14

TELEPHONE MESSAGE

TO: <u>PHIL N. URRNAMEHERE</u>

FROM: <u>MARSHALL LAWW</u>

COMPANY: <u>DEPARTMENT OF DIVERSITY TRAINING</u>

TELEPHONE NUMBER: <u>555-4627</u>

_____ **WILL CALL BACK**

__X_ **PLEASE CALL**

REGARDING: *MR. LAWW CALLED TWICE; ONCE WHILE YOU WERE REMOVING THE DOGS FROM THE GYMNASIUM AND THEN AGAIN, WHILE YOU WERE TAKING THE NEW FAMILY ON A TOUR OF THE BUILDING. I TRIED TO KEEP HIM ON THE LINE THE SECOND TIME, UNTIL YOU RETURNED TO THE OFFICE, BUT HE SAID HE WAS TOO BUSY TO WAIT. HE WANTS YOU TO CALL HIM AS SOON AS POSSIBLE AND NO LATER THAN 5:00 P.M. TODAY. HE SAID THAT HE HAS A PRESS CONFERENCE SCHEDULED FOR 10:00 A.M. TOMORROW, WHEN HE WILL ANNOUNCE THE RESULTS OF A RECENT DDT COMMUNITY SURVEY. HE SAID THE RESULTS DEMONSTRATE THAT OUR SCHOOL (AND HERE HE INSISTED THAT I RECORD HIS MESSAGE WORD FOR WORD!) "(1) FAILS TO GIVE ANY CREDENCE TO THE VALUES OR OPINIONS HELD BY INDIVIDUALS OR GROUPS THAT CONFLICT WITH EACH OTHER OR THE SCHOOL NORM AND (2) FAILS TO RECOGNIZE AND VALUE DIVERSITY." MR. LAWW SAID IF YOU HAVE EVIDENCE TO THE CONTRARY, HE WOULD WELCOME YOUR FEEDBACK, BEFORE HE ISSUES HIS STATEMENT TO THE MEDIA TOMORROW.*

—IMA

P.S. YOU MAY ALREADY KNOW THIS: ACCORDING TO ONE OF OUR CAFETERIA WORKERS WHO IS RELATED TO ONE OF THE SCHOOL DISTRICT'S BUS DRIVERS, THERE IS A RUMOR GOING AROUND THE "BUS BARN" THAT MARSHALL LAWW WILL BE RUNNING FOR THE SCHOOL BOARD NEXT YEAR.

MODULE 27: **167**
PROMOTE
YOUR MENTEE'S
PROFESSIONAL
GROWTH
THROUGH
ISLLC-BASED
SCENARIOS

Discussion Prompts Related to the Telephone Message From Marshall Laww, as Noted by Secretary Ima Wise

1. As the principal, would you respond to this telephone message? Explain your answer.

2. If you choose to respond, how would you respond—in writing, by telephone, in person, or through a designee—and when would you respond?

3. Would you seek additional information before responding? If "yes," what additional information would you seek?

4. According to Ima's notes, Marshall Laww has imposed a tight time frame around your opportunity to respond. Do you acknowledge his time constraints? What, if anything, do you make of Marshall's insistence that Ima record his message word for word? If you choose to defend the school's performance record in acknowledging different opinions and valuing diversity, what "evidence to the contrary" could you cite?

5. If you foresee issues in this scenario that might develop in the future, please identify them. (Hint: look for two possibilities in Ima's "P.S.")

6. This scenario relates to ISLLC Standard 4. If you see a connection between this scenario and other ISLLC Standards, please explain the connection.

7. What artifacts might you collect as, or after, you resolve the situation depicted in the scenario that would serve as evidence of your leadership?

Scenario 15

Errey Funeral Home
321 Woefull Way
Urrtown, Urrstate

Phil N. Urrnamehere
Principal, Urrtown School

Dear Phil:

When Superintendent DeMann and the Board of Education announced at the board meeting last week that Urrtown Schools will place a 6-mill tax levy on the next ballot, I immediately and enthusiastically volunteered to coordinate the School Levy Organizational Workers. As coordinator of the S.L.O.W. group, I will do everything in my power to promote the passage of this levy. As I told "I.B." when I volunteered, under my leadership, we will *bury* the opposition!

To get this levy passed, it is vital that I gain the support of all leaders from the business community. I want to demonstrate the interconnectedness of the community as a whole. I want the voters to understand how the success of the school system relies on the business climate in our community and vice versa. To that end, please send me a detailed list of partnerships that you have in place with area businesses, institutions of higher education, and community groups. I also would like to know how you utilize community resources to help your school solve problems and achieve goals. Also, are there any community youth or family services programs that are integrated with the school's programs?

I eagerly await your assistance in these matters.

—Mort U. Errey
Director of Services
Errey Funeral Home

MODULE 27: **169**
PROMOTE
YOUR MENTEE'S
PROFESSIONAL
GROWTH
THROUGH
ISLLC-BASED
SCENARIOS

Discussion Prompts Related
to the Letter From Mort U. Errey

1. As the principal, would you respond to this letter? Explain your answer.

2. If you choose to respond, how would you respond—in writing, by telephone, in person, or through a designee—and when would you respond?

3. Would you seek additional information before responding? If "yes," what additional information would you seek?

4. Mort U. Errey has shown enthusiastic willingness to solicit support for the school levy among area businesses. If few school-business partnerships in fact exist, how do you explain that to Mort? If numerous school-business partnerships do exist, how do you maintain them, given the multitude of tasks that you face as a new principal? In other words, how do you balance the activities associated with out-of-school organizations and the day-to-day demands of the job?

5. If you foresee issues in this scenario that might develop into future pitfalls, please identify them.

6. This scenario relates to ISLLC Standard 4. If you see a connection between this scenario and other ISLLC Standards, please explain the connection.

7. What artifacts might you collect as, or after, you resolve the situation depicted in the scenario that would serve as evidence of your leadership?

Scenario 16

URRTOWN SCHOOL DISTRICT
OFFICE OF THE SUPERINTENDENT

Mr. I. B. DeMann, Superintendent

TO: All principals
RE: Collaboration between the schools and the community

As our school district embarks on the upcoming levy campaign, it occurs to me that our administrative team ought to assess the amount of collaboration that exists between the schools and the community. We need to determine how effectively we are interacting with the entire community and react accordingly.

Here are two basic points that I strongly endorse:

1. It is essential that we provide a comprehensive community relations program that centers on having all district administrators maintain high visibility in the community.

2. Our administrators need to be actively involved in the community, and they must demonstrate that they perceive communication with the larger community as a priority.

Please take stock of your operation in this area, and be prepared to describe and discuss your performance in the upcoming evaluation conference that I am to conduct with each of you. I will have my secretary call and arrange an appointment with you. If, during your evaluation conference, I determine it to be necessary or appropriate, I will direct you to write a goal statement regarding your efforts in this vital area of school administration.

—IBD

MODULE 27: **171**
PROMOTE
YOUR MENTEE'S
PROFESSIONAL
GROWTH
THROUGH
ISLLC-BASED
SCENARIOS

Discussion Prompts Related to the Memo From I. B. DeMann

1. As the principal, would you respond to this memo? Explain your answer.

2. If you choose to respond, how would you respond—in writing, by telephone, in person, or through a designee—and when would you respond?

3. Would you seek additional information before responding? If "yes," what additional information would you seek?

4. What are the implications for the building principal when the superintendent expresses the expectation that all district administrators "maintain high visibility in the community" and "demonstrate that they perceive communication with the larger community as a priority"? Does the timing of this memo cause you any concern? Do you have any concern as to how the superintendent will determine if it is "necessary or appropriate" to have you adopt a goal in this area?

5. If you foresee issues in this scenario that might develop into future pitfalls, please identify them.

6. This scenario relates to ISLLC Standard 4. If you see a connection between this scenario and other ISLLC Standards, please explain the connection.

7. What artifacts might you collect as, or after, you resolve the situation depicted in the scenario that would serve as evidence of your leadership?

Scenario 17

Urrtown High School
Debate Club
"Constantly Cultivating Controvertible Conversations"

Dear Principal Urrnamehere:

Our debate club is preparing for competition at the regional debate tournament, and the initial prompt for this year's contest is the general topic of "Values, Beliefs, and Attitudes in the Workplace."

We are engaged in the process of contacting executives and managers of companies and organizations to gather ideas about this topic. It occurred to us that school principals must work with the values, beliefs, and attitudes of many different people from many different occupations and walks of life. For this reason, we are contacting all principals in the Urrtown School District and asking that you and your colleagues share ideas with us on the following points:

1. In what way do you demonstrate or model values, beliefs, and attitudes that inspire others to higher levels of performance?

2. How are the central values of our diverse school community considered by the school administration when making decisions about the operation of the school?

We realize that you are very busy, but we greatly value and appreciate your insight on this topic. We hope you will find the time, energy, and interest necessary to respond to our questions.

—*Grant A. Woosh, President*
Urrtown High School Debate Club

MODULE 27: **173**
PROMOTE
YOUR MENTEE'S
PROFESSIONAL
GROWTH
THROUGH
ISLLC-BASED
SCENARIOS

Discussion Prompts Related to the Letter From Grant A. Woosh

1. As the principal, would you respond to this letter? Explain your answer.

2. If you choose to respond, how would you respond—in writing, by telephone, in person, or through a designee—and when would you respond?

3. Would you seek additional information before responding? If "yes," what additional information would you seek?

4. Identify what you consider the best way that you, as an entry-year principal, can "demonstrate or model values, beliefs, and attitudes that inspire others to higher levels of performance."

5. If you foresee issues in this scenario that might develop into future pitfalls, please identify them.

6. This scenario relates to ISLLC Standard 5. If you see a connection between this scenario and other ISLLC Standards, please explain the connection.

7. What artifacts might you collect as, or after, you resolve the situation depicted in the scenario that would serve as evidence of your leadership?

Scenario 18

MARY WHEY
808 VALLEY VISTA DRIVE
URRTOWN, URRSTATE

Dear Phil,

How about a no-expense stay in a three-bedroom condo in Ft. Myers, Florida, over the spring vacation for you and your family? No, this is not some weird sales promotion. This is a real, legitimate, no-strings-attached offer from your friendly PTO president!

My family has this wonderful, first-class, time-share condo *right on the beach* that we have used during spring vacation over the past four years. But this year we are going to stay in the Bahamas with my husband's older brother at no expense to us. So, we can easily afford to share our good fortune and offer this great opportunity to you. My husband and I thought of you and your family because we see how hard you work at the various PTO projects throughout the school year. We have not told, nor will we tell, our children about offering the condo to you. So you do not need to be concerned about the slightest appearance of impropriety; no one else will know. My husband and I believe that, as the saying goes, "you deserve a break today," and today, this is yours! (And, with two younger children still to come through your building, we may be able to extend this offer to you again.)

I would have called you to discuss this in person, but I must leave this afternoon on a two-week college reunion trip and I did not want to delay asking you until I returned. Please leave a message on my machine saying, "Yes!" We can talk in two weeks about the particulars.

Best wishes,
—Mary

MODULE 27: **175**
PROMOTE
YOUR MENTEE'S
PROFESSIONAL
GROWTH
THROUGH
ISLLC-BASED
SCENARIOS

Discussion Prompts Related to the Letter From Mary Whey

1. As the principal, would you respond to this letter? Explain your answer.

2. If you choose to respond, how would you respond—in writing, by telephone, in person, or through a designee—and when would you respond?

3. Would you seek additional information before responding? If "yes," what additional information would you seek?

4. If you foresee issues in this scenario that might develop into future pitfalls, please identify them. If you need a hint, consider Mary's statements, "a no-strings-attached offer" and "with two younger children still to come through your building, we may be able to extend this offer to you again."

5. Would you respond differently if Mary (or any other parent) offered a similar opportunity to a teacher on the staff?

6. This scenario relates to ISLLC Standard 5. If you see a connection between this scenario and other ISLLC Standards, please explain the connection.

7. What artifacts might you collect as, or after, you resolve the situation depicted in the scenario that would serve as evidence of your leadership?

Scenario 19

PHIL LANGEES, M.D.
Specializing in Hand Surgery Since 1996
Urrtown Medical Center
10 Metacarpal Blvd.
Urrtown, Urrstate

To all Urrtown building principals:

As you may realize, I am the chairperson of the local chapter of the nationally recognized Citizens for Honest Appraisals and Observations of Schools. The CHAOS mission is to provide accurate and credible input to the school administration regarding the effectiveness of the school program as perceived by the citizens of Urrtown. We are quite committed to our charge; our motto is "CHAOS will prevail!"

Near the end of the past school year, our CHAOS chapter conducted a telephone survey to collect data pertinent for our study of the school district's effectiveness. As a companion piece to the telephone survey, we will now conduct on-site visitations to scrutinize the actual day-to-day operations of the schools. This letter is to inform you that I will call next week to discuss our visit to your school. Since we are in the formative stages of designing the evaluation instrument that our committee members will use during their school visits, I am open to discussing the nature and scope of the committee's visit and observation.

I sincerely hope that your willingness to open your building to such public scrutiny will be enthusiastic and unlimited. I thank you in advance for your cooperation.

Sincerely,
—Phil Langees, M.D.

MODULE 27: **177**
PROMOTE
YOUR MENTEE'S
PROFESSIONAL
GROWTH
THROUGH
ISLLC-BASED
SCENARIOS

Discussion Prompts Related
to the Letter From Phil Langees

1. As the principal, would you respond to this letter? Explain your answer.

2. If you choose to respond, how would you respond—in writing, by telephone, in person, or through a designee—and when would you respond?

3. If you choose to respond, would you seek additional information before responding? If "yes," what additional information would you seek?

4. If you foresee issues in this scenario that might develop into future pitfalls, please identify them.

5. This scenario relates to ISLLC Standard 5. If you see a connection between this scenario and other ISLLC Standards, please explain the connection.

6. What artifacts might you collect as, or after, you resolve the situation depicted in the scenario that would serve as evidence of your leadership?

Scenario 20

```
<<<EMAILER.ROUTED_PER_93880.COM>>>
SUBJ: "RUMOR MILL"
DATE:07/07/01
FROM: NEAL DOWNE
TO:PHIL N. URRENAMEHERE
```

PHIL: EVER SINCE THE TIME I KNELT DOWN TO PLACE
THE FOOTBALL SO THAT HUGH MONGUSS (WHAT A BIG MAN
ON CAMPUS HE WAS!) COULD KICK THE WINNING FIELD
GOAL AGAINST BOONEYVILLE FOR THE LEAGUE
CHAMPIONSHIP, I HAVE FELT A SPECIAL KINSHIP FOR
URRTOWN SCHOOLS.

MY LOYALTY AND CONCERN FOR THE SCHOOL SYSTEM
COMPELS ME TO SHARE A RUMOR THAT I HEARD THIS
MORNING AT THE GAS AND GULP OUT ON PETERSON PIKE.
AFTER SOME WORKERS FROM A SURVEY CREW FINISHED
FILLING UP ON GAS AND COFFEE AND HIT THE ROAD, THE
STORE MANAGER TOLD ME THAT THESE GUYS ARE SURVEYING
THE OLD GUNTLER PROPERTY ON ROUTE 13. THE
POTENTIALLY GOOD NEWS: HE SAID THE SURVEY CREW IS
WORKING FOR SOME CANADIAN COMPANY THAT IS GOING TO
BUILD A LARGE FOOD-PROCESSING PLANT THAT WILL
EMPLOY OVER 500 WORKERS. THE POTENTIALLY BAD NEWS:
THE COMPANY IS IMPORTING 500 NON-ENGLISH-SPEAKING
WORKERS AND THEIR FAMILIES FROM EASTERN EUROPE.

IS THE RUMOR TRUE? WHAT ARE THE POTENTIAL ISSUES
IF THIS IS TRUE? ON A LARGER SCALE, DOES THE
SCHOOL DISTRICT HAVE CONNECTIONS THAT HELP IT STAY
ABREAST OF TRENDS, ISSUES, AND POTENTIAL CHANGES IN
THE SCHOOLS' EXTERNAL ENVIRONMENT?

THANKS, NEAL

--------------------HEADERS----------------------

RETURN PATH <NEIL.DOWNE@INCOME.NET>
RECEIVED: FROM GPXX-QWTRT.NX.USB(WEB/US)[P46P2]BY
Z-SENDER
TMPT<ID_894946MIMEVERSION:653XMAILER-RETURN TO
SENDER.COM
```
```

MODULE 27: **179**
PROMOTE
YOUR MENTEE'S
PROFESSIONAL
GROWTH
THROUGH
ISLLC-BASED
SCENARIOS

Discussion Prompts Related to the E-mail From Neal Downe

1. As the principal, would you respond to this e-mail? Explain your answer.

2. If you choose to respond, how would you respond—in writing, by telephone, in person, or through a designee—and when would you respond?

3. If you choose to respond, would you seek additional information before responding? If "yes," what additional information would you seek?

4. If you foresee issues in this scenario that might develop into future pitfalls, please identify them.

5. This scenario relates to ISLLC Standard 6. If you see a connection between this scenario and other ISLLC Standards, please explain the connection.

6. What artifacts might you collect as, or after, you resolve the situation depicted in the scenario that would serve as evidence of your leadership?

Scenario 21

Sandy Beech
Urrtown School

Dear Phil,

I wonder if you could help me. I enrolled in a school leadership course in the Department of Educational Leadership at Urrtown University, and one of my assignments is to survey district principals regarding several school leadership issues. Would you be willing to allow me to interview you?

If you consent to my request, I will stop by your office during my planning period in the next couple of days to schedule a time when we might meet.

In addition to asking you for information about how you became a building administrator, I am to ask for your response to the following question: "How does the school community work within the framework of policies, laws, and regulations enacted by local, state, and federal authorities?"

Would you kindly take a few minutes from your busy schedule and reflect on this question prior to my meeting with you? As I said previously, I will be in touch.

Thank you very much for considering my request.

—*Sandy*

MODULE 27: **181**
PROMOTE
YOUR MENTEE'S
PROFESSIONAL
GROWTH
THROUGH
ISLLC-BASED
SCENARIOS

Discussion Prompts Related to the Letter From Sandy Beech

1. As the principal, would you respond to this letter? Explain your answer.

2. If you choose to respond, how would you respond—in writing, by telephone, in person, or through a designee—and when would you respond?

3. If you choose to respond, would you seek additional information before responding? If "yes," what additional information would you seek?

4. If you foresee issues in this scenario that might develop into future pitfalls, please identify them.

5. This scenario relates to ISLLC Standard 6. If you see a connection between this scenario and other ISLLC Standards, please explain the connection.

6. What artifacts might you collect as, or after, you resolve the situation depicted in the scenario that would serve as evidence of your leadership?

Scenario 22

Roy Al Payne
4267 Tribulation Trail
Urrtown, Urrstate

Dear Principal Urrnamehere:

To assure the continued control of our public schools at the local level, I vigorously protest any affiliation between school administrators and politicians! It has come to my attention, through a longtime friend who is not only a school district employee but also a very reliable and trusted source, that certain school administrators are actively pursuing relationships with elected officials at the state level. (In other words, she knows that telephone conversations occur *on school time* between school leaders and politicians while they make plans about traveling to the state capital to "testify" at committee meetings and eat fancy lunches or meeting at state parks to talk "business" over 18 holes of golf.

I understand that school administrators operate within the framework of policies, laws, and regulations enacted by local, state, and federal authorities. However, school leaders should not be "palsy-walsy" with politicians. Yes, elected officials can come into the classroom to talk about the political process and civic duties; however, it should stop there! I can think of no good reason for any of our school leaders to be "developing lines of communication" with decision makers outside our school community. We pay our school employees to work here and they should stay here! Do not tell me about staying on top of "pending legislation." We elect school board members to deal with those kinds of issues. School employees should stay out of politics—and stay on the job, where they belong!

Respectfully submitted,
—Roy A. Payne

P.S. I wrote to you because my source works in *your* school.

MODULE 27: **183**
PROMOTE
YOUR MENTEE'S
PROFESSIONAL
GROWTH
THROUGH
ISLLC-BASED
SCENARIOS

Discussion Prompts Related to the Letter From Roy Al Payne

1. As the principal, would you respond to this letter? Explain your answer.

2. If you choose to respond, how would you respond—in writing, by telephone, in person, or through a designee—and when would you respond?

3. Would you seek additional information before responding? If "yes," what additional information would you seek?

4. If you foresee issues in this scenario that might develop into future pitfalls, please identify them. For example, what are the implications of Roy's closing remark?

5. This scenario relates to ISLLC Standard 6. If you see a connection between this scenario and other ISLLC Standards, please explain the connection.

6. What artifacts might you collect as, or after, you resolve the situation depicted in the scenario that would serve as evidence of your leadership?

28 Help Your Mentee Prepare to Document Her or His Leadership

In addition to helping your mentee realize the importance of growing on the job, you can guide her or him toward becoming a higher-performing professional educator. You might begin by encouraging your mentee to assume greater responsibility for developing a personal plan of professional development. One facet of such a plan involves relicensure.

Assuming that your mentee is successful and desires to continue serving in the realm of school leadership, she or he will face the task of renewing her or his principal's license. I encourage you to reflect on ways that you can help your mentee think about demonstrating professional growth and ultimately acquiring a renewed or upgraded license.

Increasingly, as a part of the relicensure process, the principal must show evidence of professional growth. Whether demonstrated with a portfolio, an oral presentation, an on-site visitation, or some other form of validation, the principal's proof of professional growth and access to relicensure is now—or likely will be in the future—determined by job performance in relation to established standards. As reflected in the report titled "ISLLC Projects and Participating States," the ISLLC Standards are gaining increasing acceptance as the "industry standard" for validating professional development (CCSSO, 1996). Should you help your entry-year mentee *get ready* to demonstrate such professional growth in relation to the ISLLC Standards? I contend that you should, and I offer the following suggestions to help you do so.

- Promote procrastination, specifically for this one point. Remember, and remind your mentee, that *the entry year is not the time* to write a portfolio

MODULE 28: **185**
HELP YOUR
MENTEE PREPARE
TO DOCUMENT
HER OR HIS
LEADERSHIP

or develop an oral presentation or prepare for an on-site evaluation team. Primarily, you want your mentee to *think about getting ready* to do that kind of activity after concluding the first year. The operative phrase in the preceding sentence is "think about getting ready," which leads to the next point, the "gradual collection."

• Think "gradual collection." Encourage your mentee to get ready to produce evidence of performance as a school leader by gathering items during the entry year that reflect her or his role in various aspects of the school's operation. This is the "gradual collection" concept—routinely collecting artifacts from the day-to-day activities to validate the principal's leadership in relation to the ISLLC Standards. Remind your mentee that this gradual collection continues beyond the entry year, as the principal may collect and select items until she or he has assembled a demonstration of performance.

• File early and file often. Advise your mentee to adopt an organized approach for gathering *and filing* artifacts; suggest creating six files, whether folders, notebooks, boxes, or buckets, and labeling them with the ISLLC Standards. Then, as your mentee collects various artifacts, they can be filed more efficiently, which facilitates reviewing and choosing among them in the future. In addition, it is wise for the mentee to record some notes when filing a particular artifact that explain why the mentee thought particular items were worth keeping. Such notes serve as "memory joggers" when the mentee later reviews the documentation files.

• Suggest what qualifies as appropriate artifacts. The appropriateness of an artifact depends on how the principal integrates it into a presentation of professional growth. If the principal clearly explains how the artifact reflects her or his leadership in relation to a particular standard, then the artifact is appropriate. At first, your mentee may need assistance in recognizing potential artifacts. You may create your own list of appropriate artifacts to share with your mentee, or you and your mentee may mutually create such a list; or you may draw from the list of examples that appears in Tables 22-27.

RECOMMENDED READINGS RELATED TO "MENTORING THE MENTOR"

Of the five mentoring resources listed on page 172, one provides advice specifically related to the school setting. *Leaders Helping Leaders*, by John Daresh, provides direction for school district leaders when designing and implementing an administrator-mentoring program. In addition to relevant information, he provides self-check quizzes and scenarios for reflective thought.

The other books on the list, while grounded in the business world, offer valuable insights for educators who want to learn more about the mentoring, or "coaching," process. Hargrove's text, *Masterful Coaching*,

Table 22

Examples of artifacts that validate the principal's leadership in activities related to ISLLC Standard 1

ISLLC STANDARD 1: A school administrator is an educational leader who promotes the success of all students by facilitating the development, articulation, implementation, and stewardship of a vision of learning that is shared and supported by the community.

- Copy of the school's mission statement or photographs of the posted mission statement
- A copy or sections of the school's Continuous Improvement Plan
- Copy of posted rules, expectations, and goals
- Samples of agendas, minutes, and membership lists of committees
- Copies of grant applications
- Copy of the building "Report Card"
- Copy of the school's Strategic Plan
- Samples of the school newsletter; reprints of the school's Web site
- Copies of community survey instrument(s); results from surveys
- Pictures of the school's marquee (various messages)

Table 23

Examples of artifacts that validate the principal's leadership in activities related to ISLLC Standard 2

ISLLC STANDARD 2: A school administrator is an educational leader who promotes the success of all students by advocating, nurturing, and sustaining a school culture and instructional program conducive to student learning and staff professional growth.

- Records of student test scores that reflect improvement
- Documents that verify the provision of programs to improve student performance
- Schedules of classes and other records that display inclusionary practices
- Documents that verify the existence of recognition programs
- Lists of rewards given to students who demonstrate desirable behavior
- Documents that verify the existence of conflict resolution programs
- Records of student and staff involvement in decision making
- Records that verify that teachers plan and deliver learning activities in a variety of teaching styles to accommodate the various learning styles of the students
- Records that show staff and principal participation in professional development activities (building, district, and beyond)
- Documents that display instructional leadership (memos, articles shared, conferences attended, and initiatives supported)

MODULE 28: **187**
HELP YOUR
MENTEE PREPARE
TO DOCUMENT
HER OR HIS
LEADERSHIP

Table 24

Examples of artifacts that validate the principal's leadership in activities related to ISLLC Standard 3

<u>ISLLC STANDARD 3</u>: A school administrator is an educational leader who promotes the success of all students by ensuring management of the organization, operations, and resources for a safe, efficient, and effective learning environment.

- Copies or sections of handbooks—student, parent, staff, volunteers
- Survey results that reflect feelings of staff, students, and community about safety and academic progress
- Records that verify staff, student, and parent representation in the operation of the school; including a problem-solving system
- Records that display scheduled, internal audits of the work environment
- Records of communications to all school stakeholders and staff that enhance school organization (building schedules, daily bulletins, reminder memos, calendars regarding upcoming events and dates)
- Documents that display an active parent-teacher organization (agendas and minutes of meetings, budget statements, newsletters)
- Records that display a proactive and positive public relations effort toward the community (parent-teacher organization, newsletters, flyers, Web site, telephone "hot line," committees, Open Houses, outreach programs)

---

provides a two-pronged approach: coaching individuals and coaching groups. Fournies takes a results-oriented view of coaching, with emphasis on getting the most out of each employee. Bell's book is an easy-to-read text with numerous examples of mentoring techniques and success stories.

* * *

Bell, C. (1996). *Managers as Mentors: Building Partnerships for Learning.* San Francisco: Berrett-Koehler.

Daresh, J. C. (2001). *Leaders Helping Leader—A Practical Guide to Administrative Mentoring.* Thousand Oaks, CA: Corwin.

Fournies, F. F. (2000). *Coaching for Improved Work Performance.* New York: McGraw-Hill.

Goldsmith, M., Lyons, L., & Freas, A. (Eds). (2000). *Coaching for Leadership.* San Francisco: Jossey-Bass/Pfeiffer.

Hargrove, R. (1995). *Masterful Coaching: Extraordinary Results by Transforming People and the Way They Think and Work Together.* San Francisco: Jossey-Bass/Pfeiffer.

Table 25

Examples of artifacts that validate the principal's leadership in activities related to ISLLC Standard 4

ISLLC STANDARD 4: A school administrator is an educational leader who promotes the success of all students by collaborating with families and community members, responding to diverse community interests and needs, and mobilizing community resources.

- Records verifying student community service and volunteer programs
- Records that display performance programs within the community
- Evidence of students' participation in diversity activities (plays, workshops)
- Printed programs associated with events that promote diversity
- Records that display staff involvement at community events
- Records verifying staff involvement in community clubs, groups, and projects
- Records that display the use of the school facilities by community groups
- Records that display the school's efforts to access and use the talents of community members as resource speakers
- Records that display the existence and proactive use of a diverse, broad-based Principal's Advisory Committee
- Records that verify the involvement of community members in curriculum review or revision

MODULE 28: **189**
HELP YOUR
MENTEE PREPARE
TO DOCUMENT
HER OR HIS
LEADERSHIP

Table 26

Examples of artifacts that validate the principal's leadership in activities related to ISLLC Standard 5

ISLLC STANDARD 5: A school administrator is an educational leader who promotes the success of all students by acting with integrity, fairness, and in an ethical manner.

- Records that confirm and display the use of a conflict resolution process
- Records of surveys that confirm student satisfaction with fair and ethical treatment and their involvement in decision making
- Copies of the school's mission statement that express an expectation that all staff members act with integrity, fairness, and in an ethical manner
- Records of survey instruments and survey results that confirm community, student, and staff satisfaction with the ethical environment and atmosphere at the school
- Records of internal audits that confirm the curriculum is equitable, diverse, and multicultural
- Records that display the regular use of a process for community input
- Survey instruments and results that display the community's satisfaction with the ethics and fairness of the principal's decisions and actions
- Records that verify the regularly scheduled celebration of diversity through holidays, events, and celebrations

Table 27

Examples of artifacts that validate the principal's leadership in activities related to ISLLC Standard 6

<u>ISLLC STANDARD 6</u>: A school administrator is an educational leader who promotes the success of all students by understanding, responding to, and influencing the larger political, social, economic, legal, and cultural context.

- Records that verify a planned effort by school leadership to keep the community informed and updated on state and federal initiatives, regulations, and standards
- Records that verify the involvement of the principal in educational and community organizations
- Evidence of programs related to global issues
- Evidence of citizen education programs
- Notes and summaries from labor-management meetings
- Evidence of efforts to monitor and influence school-related legislation
- Notes and summaries from parent and community advisory committee meetings
- Records that confirm community representatives serve on building or district committees for short- and long-range planning and goal-setting forums
- Documents that confirm community involvement in curriculum review, revision, or adoption

REFERENCES

Bennis, W. G. (1989). *On Becoming a Leader.* Reading, MA: Addison-Wesley.

Council of Chief State School Officers. (1996). *ISLLC Projects and Participating States,* Retrieved October 22, 2002, from http://www.ccsso.org/pdfs/isllc-chart00.pdf

Council of Chief State School Officers. (1996). *Standards for School Leaders.* Retrieved October 22, 2002, from http://www.ccsso.org/standrds.html

Murphy, J. F. (2002, September/October). How the ISLLC Standards are Reshaping the Principalship. *The Principal, 82*(1), 22–25.

Riggins, C. G. (2002, September/October) Balancing Instruction and Management. *The Principal, 82*(1), 8.

Sergiovanni, T. J. (1992). *Moral Leadership: Getting to the Heart of School Improvement.* San Francisco: Jossey-Bass.

Webster's New World College Dictionary (4th ed.). (2000). Foster City, CA: IDG Books.

Index

**CORWIN
PRESS**

The Corwin Press logo—a raven striding across an open book—represents the happy union of courage and learning. We are a professional-level publisher of books and journals for K-12 educators, and we are committed to creating and providing resources that embody these qualities. Corwin's motto is "Success for All Learners."